Universal Decimal Classification (IME-1993) (Theory and Practice)

A Self Instructional Manual

Prof. A.A.N. Raju
Formerly Head,
Dept. of Library and Information Science
Osmania University, Hyderabad - 500 007

Ess Ess Publications

4837/24, Ansari Road, Darya Ganj,
New Delhi-110002
✆ : 23260807, 41563444
Fax : 011-41563334
E-mail: info@essessreference.com
url:http://www.essessreference.com

First Published **2007**

ISBN: 81-7000-501-9

Rs. 800/-

Published by:
Ess Ess Publications
4837/24, Ansari Road, Darya Ganj, New Delhi-110 002
Tel: 011-23260807, 41563444 Fax: 011-41563334
E-mail: info@essessreference.com
url: www.essessreference.com

Printed in India at:
Printline, New Delhi

CONTENTS

PREFACE

Universal Decimal Classification (UDC) is one of the most important and widely used general schemes of library classification. The scheme is taught both in theory and practice at Masters degree level in the Indian LIS Schools and most of the foreign LIS Schools as well especially in the European Continent.

The present work on UDC (IME-93) consists of two blocks viz. Block-1: Theoretical aspects of UDC and Block-2: Practical Classification with UDC (IME-93). Block-1 deals with the genesis and development of UDC and features of International Medium Edition-1993 (IME-93). Block-2 deals with common and special auxiliary tables, synthesis or number building process and classification of titles falling under the main classes 0/9 with UDC (IME-93).

An effort has been made to present the theory and practice in self-instructional mode keeping in view the requirements of the students of conventional universities as well as distance learners of Open Universities, Distance and Correspondence Educational Institutes in the Country and abroad, which are offering LIS programes at undergraduate and postgraduate levels.

In Block-2 practical classification with IME-93 very exhaustive treatment has been given to the use of common and special auxiliaries and classification of simple, compound and complex titles falling under different subject fields. While constructing the class number for a specific title, step by step analysis has been attempted to indicate the occurrence of different facets indicating the respective notation taken from the schedules and auxiliary tables and synthesizing various facets to arrive at co-extensive class number with respective connecting symbols. This method of step by step analysis and synthesis facilitates the learning process and helps in sustaining the cognitive, affective and psychomotor domains of traditional as well as distance learners.

Each Unit provides for necessary access devices such as: aims and objectives, introduction, section and sub-section headings, self-check exercises, summary and model answers to self check exercises to give clues to the learner to comprehend the contents, retain important points in the memory and retrieve them when needed and practice the skills he/she comprehends after going through this manual. The assignments provided for at the end of each Unit will enable the student / distance learner to classify additional titles to acquire more practice.

An effort has also been to establish linkages between sections and sub-sections within a Unit and between Units of a block to achieve continuous flow of thought throughout so as to communicate to the learner, the relevance, utility and relationship of different units and also the theoretical and practical aspects of UDC (IME-93).

The Author and Publishers fervently hope that the self-instructional manual on UDC (IME-93) will go a long way in meeting the needs of students / distance learners, teachers of LIS and also practicing librarians. Constructive and positive suggestions are solicited to improve the quality of this work in the second edition.

August 15, 2006 **- Prof. A. A. N. Raju**

Hyderabad

BLOCK 1 : THEORETICAL ASPECTS OF UDC

This is block introduces you to the genesis and development of UDC and the salient features of International Medium Edition 1993. UDC is one of the most important, popular and widely used general schemes of library classification. The scheme is being used more extensively by most of the special libraries for shelf arrangement and also by indexing and abstracting services brought out by Libraries, Information/Documentation Centres, Learned Institutions, Societies and Commercial Publishers. UDC is being taught at Masters Degree level in theory and practice by most of the LIS Schools in India and abroad. Being used world wide it has been published in whole or in part in twenty different languages to meet the requirements of Library and Information Centres.

Unit 1 : Deals briefly the genesis and development of UDC including its features, principles, structure, notation, auxiliary tables, usage and manuals for proper use of UDC.

Unit 2 : Deals with salient features of UDC (IME-93) which include structure, auxiliary tables, main tables, citation and filing order and Alphabetical Subject Index.

Unit 1
Genesis And Development of UDC

STRUCTURE

1.0. OBJECTIVES

After going through this Unit, you will be in a position to:

* trace the genesis, development, features and principles of UDC;
* understand the structure and features of notation of UDC;
* know the variety of auxiliary tables and signs employed in UDC; and
* know the wide usage of UDC and the manuals brought out for the use of UDC in Libraries and Information Centres.

1.1. INTRODUCTION

UDC is one of the most important and general schemes of library classification. The scheme was developed on the basis of Decimal Classification and first published in the year 1905 entitled *Classification Decimale Universelle* by Paul Otlet and Henri La Fontaine. This scheme is revised and updated from time to time by International Federation for Information and Documentation (FID). The scheme is very widely used in most of the Special Libraries and Information Centres and also by bibliographical services throughout the world. The scheme possess certain distinct features and notational techniques so as to meet the ever growing needs of the user libraries and information centres. Let us therefore acquaint ourselves with the features, principles, structure, qualities of notation, auxiliary tables in UDC and its wider use for classifying and systematic arrangement of documents on the shelves and entries in bibliographies, and Indexing and Abstracting Bulletins.

1.2. GENESIS AND DEVELOPMENT

The credit of using decimal fraction notation for the first time in library classification goes to Melvil Dewey, the author of *Decimal Classification* published in 1876. The value of this scheme was soon recognised and its use rapidly extended to the continent of Europe. In the year 1895 the first International Conference on Bibliography was held in Brussels. As a result of this Conference, Institute International de Bibliographic (IIB) was founded. During the course of its history, the Institute changed its name twice. In 1931 it was changed to Institute International de Documentation (IID). Again in 1937 the Institute assumed the present name of Federation International de Documentation (FID). The FID General Assembly in Montreal, 1986 agreed to make change by incorporating the word 'Information'. In future it will be known as International Federation for Information and Documentation although the acronym FID will continue to be used.

The Institute sponsored a scheme initiated by two Belgian enthusiasts Paul Otlet and Henri La Fontaine for the establishment of a comprehensive classified Index to all published information to which people all over the world would contribute and which would in turn be available to all. After examining the existing systems Otlet and La Fontaine concluded that Dewey Decimal Classification which was then in 5th Edition offered the most suitable basis, being a purely subject classification using internationally known Indo-Arabic numbers as decimal fraction notation which offers infinite hospitality in the subdivision of a class. Otlet and La Fontaine wrote to Dewey and sought his permission to extend the detail in his scheme to make it suitable for arranging the kind of Index they had in mind. Dewey gave permission to extend the schedules on the condition that the order of the main classes and divisions be maintained and that maximum compatability in development be obtained. These two Belgians then proceeded to enlarge the schedules of DC by adding extensively to its enumerative classes. The extension provides an apparatus for synthesis or number building. In 1905 the complete International edition in French of what was later called the *Classification Decimale Universelle* was published. This edition consisted of some 33,000 subdivisions with an alphabetical Index of 38,000 entries titled as *Manuel du Repertoire Bibliographique Universal.* This provided basic classification schedules for the great card subject Index compiled in Brussels by the two Belgians.

The First World War (1914-1918) was a heavy blow for the activities of the Institute and it was not until the mid-twenties that work on the second edition was resumed. Otlet and La Fontaine supervised the Humanities and Social Sciences and F. Donker Duyvis supervised the Natural Sciences. From 1927 onwards, full International Editions embodying fruits of international cooperation in additions and revisions appeared in French, German and English together with numerous abridged editions in these and other languages. F. Donker Duyvis became the Secretary General of IIB in 1929 and continued in that post until his retirement in 1959. UDC as we know today owes a great deal to this great man for his tireless efforts to make it one of the great general bibliographical classification schemes. UDC found another enthusiast in S.C. Bradford, Librarian of the Science Museum Library, London. In his book on Documentation, Bradford exhaustively deals with UDC which he applied in his Library. The first work on UDC was published in English by Bradford, an abridged schedule used in theScience Museum Library entitled *Classification for Works on Pure and Applied Science in the Science Museum Library,* the third edition of which appeared in 1936. In course of time British Standards Institution (BSI) became the official British Editorial Body for bringing out UDC in English.

1.2.1. Different Editions of UDC

As pointed out earlier, the first complete edition was published in French in 1905 as *Manual du Reportoire Bibliographique Universal.* The second complete edition, also in French, was published over the years 1927-1933 had the title *Classification Decimale Universelle* an indication of the change of emphasis since the first edition. It contained some 70,000 classes enumerated in its tables and substantial alterations were made in the main classes Science and Technology. By this time it became the most detailed and flexible classification scheme ever published for use in special libraries of every kind. In 1934 the third full edition in German, entitled *Dezimal Klassification,* was begun and was completed in 1952 making it the most uptodate full edition at present in use. A three volume index was published in 1951-1953. The BSI which took the responsibility for the publication of UDC in English began in 1943, the publication of 4th edition and was expected to be completed by the end of 1977. It constitutes a British Standard BS 1000. Other full editions under preparation include revisions of the German and French editions and new ventures in Japanese 1950, and Spanish 1955, Polish 1959 and Portuguese 1961.

In addition to the above mentioned full editions, abridged editions of the whole UDC have been published in 13 different languages. The First British abridged edition was published in 1948, the second edition in 1957 and third edition in 1961. Multilingual edition BS 1000B in German, English and French was published in 1958. These are three separate Indexes. A supplement to this has been published covering the years 1958 to 1968. Another development in the publication of UDC was the bringing out of medium editions and special subject editions. Medium edition first published in German, was intended to fall between the full and abridged editions. This medium edition contains about 30% of the full tables. The international medium editions in Geman and English versions were expected to appear in 1977 with the French editions following shortly after. But the International MediumEdition (IME) English Text was brought out by BSI in 1985 (BS 1000 M: 1985) in two parts, viz., Part 1: Systematic Tables (1985) and Part 2 Alphabetical Subject Index (1988). You please refer to Unit 2 which deals with salient features of IME. Special subject editions were brought out in Nuclear Science, Mining and Metallurgy and Building. These editions are usually based on the practice of a larger library system.

1.2.2. Organisation and Revision

The development and maintenance of UDC is the responsibility of FID. This is exercised through its international committee on which all national member committees are entitled to be represented. The overall control is vested in the Central Classification Committee FID/CCC consisting of FID Secretary General and editors of full editions of UDC. Each member nation of FID may have its own national committee for bringing out editions in the language of that country. In addition to these committees there are national and international subject committees. The International Committee report to the FID/CCC and the national subject committees report to the national committees.

Proposal for revision or extension generally comes from the users of UDC. A proposal forwarded through the national committee or by individual users is first considered by the editors who are in constant touch with FID office at the Hague where an uptodate minute master copy of the complete UDC is maintained. The proposals are then sent to the headquarters where they are studied carefully to see that it does not clash with any existing or proposed schedules. If the proposal is accepted it is published as a P-note. These proposed alterations are made public and lie on the table for four months during which time any user of UDC may comment on them. If no comments are received during this four month period, the proposal is deemed to be accepted and the schedule becomes part of UDC. Every year P-notes which have been accepted are cumulated into the 'Extensions and corrections to the UDC', and published every six months. These six monthly publications of P-notes are progressively cumulated into three year volumes. The process of revision in UDC is continuous and it is both a source of strength and weakness. The new schedules proposed by the user is scrutinised by FID/CCC to ensure that the proposals are sound from the classification point of view. The procedure that is followed,before accepting any proposed schedule as official, is a long drawn affair. It takes nearly between two to ten years for accepting a proposal and in the dynamic and fast growing disciplines like Sciences and Technologies the proposed schedules tend to become out of date before they are accepted as official and incorporated in the master schedule of UDC.

1.2.3. Management of UDC

The UDC managed by the organisation founded by Otlet and La Fontaine known since 1937 as the Federation International de Documentation (FID). The official languages of FID are English, French and German. FID works in close cooperation with various national organisations which in turn have various consultative arrangements with users of the scheme. The classification division of FID maintains a complete master version of UDC which consists of the text of the French edition of 1927-33.

The published editions of UDC in various languages are issued by the member organisations in various countries with the authority of FID. The Scheme is under continuous revision. The proposed amendments known as P-notes are circulated by FID to subscribers for comments and suggestions. The suggestions and amendments received from the users and experts are considered by the FID. The accepted suggestions, amendments will become the authorised versions of FID when published. The published amendments are incorporated into the language editions of UDC. The published amendments become known as 'Extensions and corrections'.

The English editions both full and abridged of UDC is being brought by British Standards Institution (BSI) from time to time. BSI operates a committee structure in which interested organisations are represented for formulation of revision proposals.

Self-check Exercise-1

1. Name the two Belgians who first developed UDC
2. What is the expansion of FID?
3. When the first completed edition of UDC in French was published?
4. When the first British abridged edition of UDC was published?
5. When the International Medium Edition (IME) in English was brought out?

Note:

a) Write your answers in the space given below.

b) Compare your answers with those given at the end of this Unit.

....

....

....

....

....

1.3. FEATURES AND PRINCIPLES

1.3.1 Features

It must be stated that UDC is a practical scheme based on the demands of pamphlets, reports and periodical literature rather than on the framework of a theory. Although the scheme is based on DDC, it can claim to be the first 'analytico-synthetic' library classification. It lays more stress to achieve co-extensive class number, i.e., detailed specification than the achievement of a sequence of subjects for optimum helpfulness. It avoids a lacunae of numerous private classification schemes by providing a standard system covering all the disciplines and may be used in any type of general or special library. It is a general classification scheme and it is not a bundle of special classifications but an integrated whole. The scheme reflects exhaustive enumeration in the schedules with due provision for synthesis or coordination. It is amenable to adjustments to meet special needs. This is possible because the citation order in any given class allows alternative treatments. The use of synthetic devices like Colon (:) permits coordination of concepts in different permutations, thereby minimizing the rigidity in the enumerative classification schemes. The notation in UDC is international in nature so that a file organised by it makes sense in any language. An international body for its maintenance and revision with the full cooperation of its users guarantees the continued existence of the system as a current and up-to-date one. The terminology used in UDC helps a comprehensive vocabulary of terms for indexing purpose.

1.3.2. Principles

UDC is based on the following principles:

1. It is a classification in the strict sense depending on the analysis of idea content, so that related concepts and groups of concepts are brought together and the arbitrary and often haphazard systematization of alphabetical and other arrangement is avoided.
2. It is a universal classification in that an attempt is made to include in it, every field of knowledge, not as a patch work of isolated, self-sufficient specialist groupings, but as an integrated pattern of correlated subjects.
3. It is a universal decimal classification constructed on the principle of proceeding from general to the more particular by (arbitrary) division of the whole of human knowledge into ten main branches, each further sub-divided decimally to the required degree.
4. It is essentially a practical system for retrieval of information in which the order of subjects is not of much importance than the provision for detailed specification.
5. It also accepts the principle of mutually exclusive classes, collocation of related subjects and consistency of approach.
6. To a certain extent it has tried to remove national and racial bias by removing these factors and preferring common facets. But still it is an essentially western-oriented system. It neglects oriental religious systems, philosophies, cultures and Social Sciences.
7. Its notation consists of Indo-Arabic Numerals used decimally which allows infinite hospitality to subordinate classes.
8. It employs certain notational techniques by which it is possible to link simple main class either with other main

number or with auxiliaries indicating place, time and similar commonly used categories.

1.4 STRUCTURE

As this scheme is based on DC the order of main classes and main divisions is almost the same as in the latter scheme. The notation is slightly different and there is no three figure minimum in UDC. Thus 5 is Science, 53 is Physics and 531 Mechanics. The outline of the main classes denoted by decimal fractions is as follows:

.0 Generalities : Methodology, Documentation, Scripts, etc.,

.1 Philosophy, Metaphysics, Logic, Ethics. Psychology.

.2 Religion, Theology.

.3 Social Sciences; including Statistics; Law, Education.

.4 Philology, Languages, Linguistics.

.5 Pure Science, Mathematical and Natural.

.6 Applied Science; Medicine and Technology.

.7 The arts, including Architecture, Photography, Entertainment and Sports.

.8 Literature, Belles Letters.

.9 Geography, Biography, History.

After the publication of International Medium Edition (IME) in 1985, the main class Linguistics has been transferred to Literature main class 8. In the outline of main classes the final zero is not used to give three figure minimum. In certain cases, it is used with some meaning.

e.g., 3 Social Sciences

33 Political economy, Economics

330 General concepts of Economics

1.5 NOTATION

The notation consists of Indo-Arabic numerals used decimally. In addition, several other signs are used to introduce common facets. The classes are divided from general to specific. The following example will reflect this process of division.

.3	Social Sciences
.34	Jurisprudence, Law, Legislation
.343	Criminal Law
.343.8	Penology
.343.81	Penitentiary establishments, institutions
.343.819	Other penitentiary establishments
.343.819.2	For women and young girls.

For the sake of convenience, the initial decimal point is omitted. A point is inserted at every three digits in the class number purely as a visual aid. When .00 and .0 auxiliaries are used in the class number or for some mnemonic purpose such as parallel division of 91 and the (4) to (9) auxiliaries, e.g., 91.44 Geography of France, the position of the point varies.

1.5.1. Qualities of Notation

The following qualities are evident in the notation of UDC. These are briefly described below:

1. ***Subordination to Order***

The notation reflects the process of division from general to specific and subordination to order. The above examples demonstrates this order. But because of enumerative nature and limited base, the class number for minute subjects is lengthy.

2. ***Simplicity***

The main schedules are derived on the basis of Indo-Arabic numerals alone. But for common auxiliaries and special auxiliaries a number of indicators were used which make the notation mixed. Thus the notation undoubtedly becomes complicated in nature. As a result of the use of several indicators, a definite ordinal value has to be awarded for each of these non-numeral symbols.

3. *Brevity*

As stated elsewhere, the notation is far from brief. This quality suffers due to small base of ten Indo-Arabic numerals as decimals and poor allocation of numbers to classes. Many class numbers in UDC exceed six digits in length. Because of poor allocation, extensive and dynamic subjects got less number of places than relatively restricted and static subjects. The purpose of several synthetic devices is to achieve co-extensive class number, and as a consequence the class numbers tend to be very lengthy.

4. *Hospitality*

A notation of the scheme should be hospitable to new subjects. There are two types of hospitality, viz., hospitality in array (coordinate classes) and hospitality in chain (subordinate classes). Hospitality in array is achieved in UDC by using 'Centesimal' device: Alphabetical device is also used, e.g., names of plants, persons, places, industrial products etc., to extend any array. Some times zero is also used to represent array of classes, e.g.: 308 Socio-graphy; 408 kinds of languages and dialects. Infinite hospitality in chain is achieved due to decimal fraction notation. This is also possible due to several synthetic devices with different signs which give the notation faceted quality.

5. *Flexibility*

Another notable quality of notation in UDC is its flexibility in the sense that it allows alternative arrangement of subjects. This quality is achieved: 1. by the use of distinct signs as facets indicators so that the facets may be in different orders, 2. the use of colon (:) as a general linking sign, 3. the use of intercalating devices — for general intercalation, ( )and" " for intercalating space and time facets, 4. the point of view numbers. The following example shows the hierarchies and flexibility in constructing class numbers using different citation orders.

63	Agriculture
632	Plant diseases, pests
632.9	Pest control
632.93	Methods
632.934	Chemical Control

e.g., Chemical control of pests in India

632.934(540)	Pests Control-Methods-Chemical Control-India
or 632.93(540)4	-do-

e.g. Chemical control of pests in India

632.934 (540)	Diseases, Pests-Control-Methods-Chemical Control-India
or 632.93(540)4	Diseases, Pests-Control-Methods-India-Chemical Control
or 632.9(540)34	-do- India-Methods-Chemical Control
or 632(540)934	Diseases, Pests-India-Methods-Chemical Control
or 63(540)2.934	Agriculture-India-Diseases, Pests-Control Methods-Chemical Control

1.5.2. Synthesis and Mnemonics

The scheme provides the most powerful synthetic apparatus available in series of common and special auxiliaries which act as systematic mnemonics. These auxiliary tables are supported by a series of signs of combinations and indicators. The following synthetic devices are employed in UDC.

Symbol	Name	Significance
+	Plus sign	Documents dealing with two subjects
	Stroke	Documents covering several topics which are consecutive in UDC

:	Colon	Relationship between two subjects
[ ]	Square Brackets	Relationship sign used when one of two subjects is obviously of secondary importance.

Common facets

=	Equal sign	Language subdivisions
(0...)	Parenthesis	Subdivisions of form
" "	Inverted Commas	Time facet
(1/9)	Parenthesis 1/9	Space facet
.00	Point double Zero	Points of view

Special auxiliaries

-	Hyphen
.0	Point Zero
'	Apostrophe

In the strict sense of the word all the above do not represent synthesis. The use of alphabetical device does not at all represent synthetic principle. But the above signs and auxiliary schedules do provide extra-notational strength for achieving coexistensive class number.

1.5.3 Starvation Policy

The notational techniques in UDC have greatly contributed to the flexibility of scheme. Its bias towards Science and Technology is clearly evident from the schedules in AEE and IME. In order to meet the requirements specially in Sciences and Technologies starvation policy has been introduced for future development of the scheme.

Starvation policy means that a piece of notation which has been superseded by a new schedule is to be left unused for ten years. After ten years the said notation can be used again with completely new meaning. Changes in the overall structure of scheme can be possible if there are vacant notation in which to be accommodated newly emerging subjects. This is the reason for transfering Class 4 Linguistics to Class 8 Literature in IME. After ten years, the vacant notation 4 can be used for new disciplines.

1.5.4. Bias in the Schedules

You are aware that UDC is based on the 5th Edition of DDC. Therefore it has inherited the basic structure with all its faults andprejudices. Considerable effort has been made by the promoters of UDC to neutralise this Western bias. But they could achieve very little success. The best example of bias in UDC is Religion main class. Christianity has been given undue importance neglecting other major and oldest religions. UDC which is intended for world wide use cannot continue with such bias, which is totally unacceptable. In the IME you will find that the digits 22/28 have been allocated for various aspects of Christianity and only 29 has been allocated for other religions of the world. The same is case with the main class Philosophy. Oriental philosophies especially branches of Indian Philosophy find no place in the schedules of AEE and IME.

1.6 AUXILIARY SCHEDULES

The auxiliary schedules provide maximum synthesis in UDC even though the bulk of the schedules are derived on the basis of enumeration. These may be divided into two groups, viz., the common auxiliaries and special auxiliaries as indicated elsewhere. These are in fact, a set of common facets and facet indicators which enable to synthesise freely than the more rigid notation in DC. The following schematic representation will give a clear view of these two types of auxiliary schedules.

UDC

Main Schedules
In which are set out:
Main divisions 0 to 9
and the various special
auxliaries such as
— .0' (Table (k))

Auxiliary Schedules
In which are set out:
connecting signs and
the common auxiliaries
(a) to (i)

Some of these auxiliaries are restricted in application while others may be used frequently.

1.7. WIDER USE OF UDC

The use of UDC is quite impressive. Its present position in Europe is remarkably encouraging. Latest figures indicate that of aworld total of some 110,000 libraries known to be using this classification, about fifty thousand of them are in USSR and another forty thousand in Poland. A scheme which has originated in Western Europe is now widely used in Eastern Europe. It is also widely used in Latin America and Japan. In France, Italy, Spain and Portugual, UDC is covering more ground especially in Technical and University Libraries. According to G.A. Lloyd, it has been estimated that some 20,000 copies of the Abridged Edition (BS 1000A) have been sold in the last 10 to 15 years, in other West and North European countries as well as in English speaking countries. In the developing countries of Asia and Africa interest in the use of UDC is steadily growing. In India many special libraries use UDC for shelf arrangement and also in Indexing and Abstracting Services.

Another important fact is that the medium edition of the UDC published in German prepared by the German Classification Committee was intended to serve as a master edition for translation into other languages. It has been further estimated that about 170,000 copies of the full edition of the schedules in English language are in the hands of various libraries and its continuing influence is considerable. The efforts made by such experts as J.E. Wright, Chairman, British Standard Institution's Committee OC/ 20/4 in keeping the schedules upto date by revision is also contributing to the widespread use of UDC by the libraries in the world. In addition to libraries and Information Centres using UDC, several Indexing and Abstracting Journals and Services use UDC. J. Mills has listed the Abstracting and Indexing Journals and services using UDC.

1.7.1. UDC in Computer Based Information Retrieval Systems

It was suggested as far back as 1934 that UDC was suitable for 'mechanical sorting'. The Royal Society's Scientific Information Conference held in 1948 noted the need to explore the potentialities of UDC in mechanized retrieval. But this suggestion did not get for the desired support for investigation and it did lie dormant in the forties and fifties. However, the research programmes which were carried out in the United States and in other countries like Britain, Germany, Denmark and Switzerland in the sixties helped UDC to be usable as indexing language for computerized control and processing of information in the fields of knowledge. The most significant research work in this respect was the American Institute of Physics UDC project under Freeman and Atherton. The resultsof this research work formed the main theme of the first seminar on UDC in mechanized retrieval system held at Copenhagen in 1968. The second seminar in this regard was held in Frankfurt in 1970. Both the seminars amply demonstrated the feasibility of using UDC as the indexing language in a mechanized system either in batch-processing or interactive mode. Other experiments carriedout during the later sixties in using UDC for special mechanical applications for example: the indexing of Geo-Science Abstracts and the maintenance of user-profiles in the metallurgical field clearly supported the use of UDC for mechanized retrieval systems.

1.7.2. UDC and UNISIST

It was thought in the FID circles of marking UDC 'Roof Scheme' under which could be hung the relevant special classifications, thesauri or descriptor lists, as well as the more detailed UDC divisions themselves for those who prefer a homogeneous UDC-based system. This concept received encouragement in the efforts to make UDC adopted as 'Switching language' for UNISIST (United Nations Information System in Science and Technology) the joint project of ICSU/UNESCO for a world scientific information system. An ASLIB study for the UNISIST stated the UDC. was found the 'least unsatisfactory' of the major existing schemes. But still there are some reservations on the part of the UNISIST to adopt UDC under its present form unless it can be presented as a concise, updated and well balanced schedule more satisfactory than the others. Eminent writers such as Jean Perrault, H. Wellisch, and F.A. Schmidt have argued the case for a radical reform. There are now two opinions about the revision of UDC. Some opine, as stated already, a thorough revision so as to meet the opportunities afforded by UNISIST and the challenges posed by mechanisation. Others want that the revision of UDC must be made slowly for streamlining and overhauling of classes in an evolutionary way rather than by a thorough overhaul of the existing structure. It is still to be seen how far UDC can be adopted by UNISIST for its Broad System of Ordering.

1.8. MANUALS FOR THE USE OF UDC

The main drawback for the use of UDC is the lack of precise rules -within scheme. The third abridged English edition provides in its general introduction some guidelines for the use of auxiliaries and compound numbers. To overcome this difficulty a very useful *Guide to Universal Decimal Classification (UDC)* has been published by the British Standards Institution (BSI) as BS 1000C 1963 compiled by J. Mills, which contains guidelines for the use of UDC with synopsis and outline of the UDC schedules. Another work of importance by the same author is *The Universal Decimal Classification* brought out by Graduate School of Library Service, Rutgers, the State University, New Brunswick (N.J.) in 1964, which briefly introduced the scheme. There are also a programmed text by J. Perrault entitled *Introduction to UDC* published in 1969, and also by H. Wellisch entitled *The Universal Decimal Classification: a Programmed Instruction Course* published in 1970.

1.9 INTERNATIONAL BIBLIOGRAPHIC CLASSIFICATION

UDC is undoubtedly the most truly international bibliographic classification. Through its auxiliary and special schedules and with several synthetic devices it clearly demonstrated its ability to achieve coextensive class numbers. No doubt, the order of collocation and unscientific structure inherited from DC reflects its drawback. Therefore, B.C. Vickery and Barbara F. Kyle in their articles have drawn attention to these drawbacks. Through the efforts of F. Donker Duyvis and other stalwarts determined revisions have been effected over the years so as to make it a truly universal scheme. Its use as a tool for organisation of knowledge embodied in macro and micro documents has been recognised and used as a 'standard'. As a potential international standard, no other scheme can compete with UDC. As stated elsewhere, several writers think that it must be developed and revised more extensively if it is to survive the challenge of newer systems for organisation of materials in special libraries. It is continuously aimed at classifying highly specialised packages of literatures, what Ranganathan has called 'micro thought'. Therefore, the pressure for its rapid and continual change is stronger than any other scheme. A.C. Fosket has presented a detailed study of the scheme stating the ways in which it might be brought up-to-date and more effective. The Decimal fraction notation, synthetic devices, exhaustive enumeration, flexibility,alternative arrangements, and lastly elaborate international machinery for maintenance and revision, enable UDC to remain the most important bibliographical classification scheme available for the libraries, both general and special, of the world.

Self-check Exercise - 2

1. What are the qualities of notation in UDC?
2. What for these symbols are used in UDC? a)/ b): c)= d) .00 and e) (1/9)
3. Which schedules provide maximum synthesis in UDC?
4. What is meant by starvation policy?
5. What is meant by UNISIST?

Note:

(a) Write your answers in the space given below.

(b) Compare your answers with those given at the end of this Unit.

....

....

....

....

....

1.10. SUMMARY

The genesis and development of UDC is an important landmark in the history of classification schemes. Even though the scheme is primarily based on DDC (5th Edition), the promoters have included several notational techniques to achieve analysis, and synthesis of a class number. The features and principles of the scheme have greatly contributed to attain international status,.

The introduction of decimal fraction notation, several signs and symbols to indicate various aspects of a subject have greatly helped the synthetic nature of the scheme. The several common and special auxiliaries provided in the scheme greatly help to achieve coextensive class numbers.

The revision and updating policy of UDC and its publication in various abridged and full editions in important languages of the world have greatly contributed for its wider use and acceptability by libraries, and information centres throughout the world.

1.11. ANSWERS TO SELF CHECK EXERCISES

Exercise 1

1. Paul Otlet and Henry La Fontaine
2. International Federation for Information and Documentation
3. 1905
4. 1948
5. 1985

Exercise 2

1. a) Subordination to order, b) Simplicity, c) Brevity d) Hospitality and e) flexibility
2. a) To represent consecutive subjects, b) Relationship of subjects, c) To represent language sub-divisions, d) Point of view and e) Places.
3. Auxiliary Schedules
4. It means that a piece of notation which has been superseded by a new schedule is to be left unused for ten years.
5. United Nations Information-Systems in Science and Technology or World Science Information Systems.

Unit 2
Features of International Medium Edition (IME - 1993)

STRUCTURE

2.0. Objectives
2.1. Introduction
2.2. Publication of International Medium Editions
    2.2.1. Layout
    2.2.2. Management of UDC
2.3. Structure of UDC
    2.3.1. Summary of Main Tables (Schedules).
2.4. Auxiliary Tables
    2.4.1. Common auxiliaries
    2.4.2. Special auxiliaries
2.5. Kinds of Common Auxiliaries
    2.5.1. Signs (Tables Ia and Ib)
    2.5.2. Subdivisions
        2.5.2.1. Independent
        2.5.2.2. Dependent
2.6. Independent auxiliary tables
    2.6.1. Language (Table Ic)
    2.6.2. Form (Table Id)
    2.6.3. Place (Table Ie)
    2.6.4. Ethnic grouping & nationality (Table If)
    2.6.5. Time (Table Ig)

2.0. OBJECTIVES

In unit 1, you have been introduced to the genesis and development of UDC. In this unit you will be introduced to salient feature of International Medium Edition (IME-1993). After going through this unit you will be able to :

* understand the salient features IME-93;
* grasp various auxiliary tables found in the scheme;
* recognise additions and changes introduced in the main tables;
* differentiate between citation order and filing order introduced in UDC; and

* use the Alphabetical subject index as a tool to access to UDC classes in the schedules.

2.1. INTRODUCTION

There are several general schemes of library classification. The most important and popular among them are : Dewey Decimal Classification (DDC), Universal Decimal Classification (UDC) and Colon Classification (CC). UDC definitely is one of the most important, useful and widely used general schemes of library classification (See Unit 1, section 1.7). As you are aware that knowledge/information is dynamic, continuous, multifaceted, multidimensional and everflowing like river Ganges. The classification schemes have to with stand the challenges posed by the developments taking place in the universe of knowledge. In order to meet the challenges the classification schemes have to be revised at regular intervals so as to make them up to date and meet the changing needs of Libraries and Information Centres (LICS). To meet the classification needs of user libraries, especially special libraries UDC is not only updated at regular intervals but also broughtout in the form of a bridged and medium editions. As a consequence of this policy International Medium Editions were published with extensive revision of the schedules and auxiliary tables.

2.2. PUBLICATION OF INTERNATIONAL MEDIUM EDITION

The British Standards Institution (BSI) is the authorised agency to bring abridged and medium additions in English language. The first International Medium Editions was published in 1987 under BS 1000 M : Part-1: Schedules, 1985 and Part 2 : Alphabetical Subject Index in 1988. These editions contain about a third of material of the full editions.

The International Medium Edition, English text, Edition 2 was published in 1993 in two parts, under BSI 1000M. Part 1 : Systematic tables. Part-2 : Alphabetical subject index. This edition was drawn directly from the Master Reference File

(MRF), the database maintained by the UDC consortium. This edition includes modifications authorised in *Extension and corrections to the UDC* (FID Publication No. 248).

An UDC entry contains three number elements viz., the class number at the left column, the class description at the right column and various amplifications such as notes, cross references and instructions for the number building. In addition to various signs and symbols provided in abiged English editions, two more new symbols : → (arrow) meaning 'see also' eg.;

334.73 cooperative companies → 347.726, 349.4222, 631.115.8; and ≅ (Parallel division) meaning 'subdivisions' have been introduced for the first time in IME-1985. These two new symbols are being continued in IME-1993. The symbol ≅ denotes parallel division which means the number proceeding ≅ may be subdivided in a manner analogous to the number following it. Eg.;

294.11 vedism 294.11 ≅ 291

Eg.; Sources of Vedism 294.11<u>8</u>

(the digit 8 is taken from 291.<u>8</u>)

2.2.1. Layout of UDC IME-93

Part 1 of UDC IME-93 is systematic tables. This part consists of Introduction at Page V, Summary of the classification at page xix, Auxiliary tables-section I: common auxiliary signs and subdivisions at page 1, Section II : Special auxiliary subdivisions at page 83. The main tables 0/9 are presented between the pages 87 and 907. As stated already Part 2 : Alphabetical subject index consisting of 531 pages.

2.2.2. Management of UDC

International Federation for Information and Document (FID) the parant body was managing the affairs of UDC since the publication first edition during the years 1904-1907 under the title "Manual du Repertoire Bibliographique Universal". In the year 1992 all the rights of UDC were transferred to UDC

Consortium (UDCC) of which FID was a founder member along with five UDC publishers including BSI. The central secretariat of the UDCC maintains the master reference file (MRF), the database of 60,000 entries. The MRF is the authoritative source for all subsequent published editions of UDC. The IME-93 is the first publication from this source. The executive committee of the UDCC manages the affairs UDC being published in various languages and at various levels.

2.3. STRUCTURE OF UDC

In UDC you will find two kinds of tables - the main and auxiliary tables which include common and special. The auxiliary tables support the main tables. The schedules of various main classes reflect the enumerative nature of the scheme. In other words the structure of UDC is hybrid of enumerative and faceted elements. The following schematic representation indicates the structure of UDC.

UDC

Tables (Main schedules) | Auxiliary Tables

The tables (main schedules) 0/9 are presented in Part 1 : Systematic tables. Summary of main tables is presented in the following subsection 2.3.1. The auxiliary tables are present in sections 2.4 to 2.8.

2.3.1. Summary of main tables (Schedules)

In UDC-IME-93 you will find the summary of main tables (schedules between page XIX and XXIV. The following is the important branches of knowledge :

0	Generalities ...
00	Prolegomena ...
01	Bibliography ...
02	Librarianship

030	Encyclopaedias
050	Serial Publications ...
06	Organisations ...
08	Polygraphies ...
09	Manuscripts ...
0	Philosophy, Psychology ...
11	Meta physics
159.9	Psychology
16	Logic ...
17	Moral philosophy. Ethics ...
2	Religion
22	The Bible
23/28	Christianity
29	Non-Christian religions
3.	Social Sciences ...
31	Sociology ...
32	Politics
33	Economics
34	Law
35	Public administration ...
36	Social work ...
37	Education
39	Ethnology. Folklore ....
[4]	Vacant
5	Mathematics and natural sciences
51	Mathematics
52	Astronomy ...
53	Physics
54	Chemistry ...
55	Earth Sciences ...

56	Palaeontology
57	Biological sciences
58	Botany
59	Zoology
6	Applied sciences ...
61	Medical sciences
62	Engineering ...
63	Agriculture ...
64	Home economics
65	Management ...
66	Chemical technology ...
67	Various industries
68	Industries ...
69	Building trade ...
7	The Arts ...
71	Physical planning ...
72	Architecture
73	Plastic arts
74	Drawing ...
75	Painting
76	Graphic arts
77	Photography
78	Music
79	Recreation ...
8	Language, Linguistics, Literature
81	Linguistics and languages
82	Literature
9	Geography, Biography, History
91	Geography ...
929	Biographical and related studies

930 Science of history ...

931 Ancient history

94 Medieval and modern history.

2.4. AUXILIARY TABLES

The most significant and innovative features in UDC is its auxiliary notation consisting signs and subdivisions which help construct compound and complex class numbers. The following sections, sub-sections deal with the treatment of auxiliaries in UDC-IME-93. You will find two kinds of auxiliary notation-common and special. The following chart reflects the variety of these auxiliary tables.

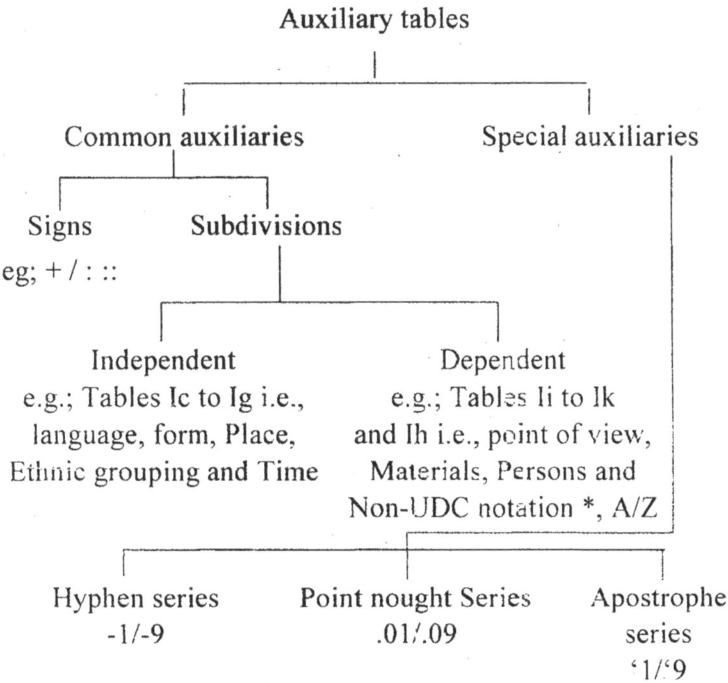

2.4.1. Common auxiliaries

The common auxiliaries denote recurrent ideas/concepts/ characteristics and are applicable throughout the scheme. These have greatly enhanced the synthetic nature or number building capacity in UDC. The table for common auxiliaries are found under section between page 1 and 82 in IME-93. A brief account of these are presented under sections 2.5 to 2.7.

2.4.2. Special auxiliaries

The special auxiliaries, as the term denotes is not listed at one place and their application is restricted or limited in nature. These appear at various places in the schedules and express concepts which are recurrent, but in a more limited subject range. The application of special auxiliaries is specified in the tables (schedules) with clear instructions and some times with worked out examples. The application of special auxiliaries is explained under Section II in IME-93 at page 83. A brief explanation with suitable examples is present consider section 2.8 of this unit.

Self Check Exercise - 1

1. In how many parts UDC-IME-93 was brought out. Name them.
2. Who is the publisher of English editions of UDC.
3. Name the type of auxiliaries found in UDC.

Note :

(a) Write your answers in the space given below :

(b) Compare your answers with the model answers given at the end of this unit .

....

....

....

2.5. KINDS OF COMMON AUXILIARIES

The universe of common auxiliaries comprise two kinds of symbols viz.; 1. signs and 2. subdivisions. These two kinds are briefly presented with suitable worked out examples in the following subsections.

2.5.1. Common auxiliary signs (Table Ia and Ib) (P. 1 and 2)

The common auxiliary signs are : + (plus), / (stroke), : (colon), [ ] (square brackets) and :: (double colon) which serve as relations for synthesising UDC members either in the schedules or auxiliary tables. But these are not themselves numbers and therefore do not represent classes and also cannot be divided further. These signs act as connecting symbols to bring two isolates or classes together. These signs have a different functions to perform in the construction of the class number. The signs + plus and / stroke are used to represent aggregation, while : colon serves to represent various relations among the isolates or classes. It does not indicate phase, intrafacet and intra-array relations as found in Colon Classification. The sign [ ] square brackets is used as subgrouping device within a complex combination, while the sign :: double colon is used to fix the order of the component number in the compound number.

Section 1 of IME-93 deals with common auxiliary signs and subdivisions (P.1). For each subsection a brief explanation has been provided.

Table Ia. Coordination, Extension

This a further divided into tow sections :

1. Coordination . Addition (sign +) and
2. Consecutive extension (sign /)

Examples :

02 + 070	Library Science and Journalism.
(540 +510)	India and China
011/016	Bibliographies.
562/569	Systematic palaeozoology.

Table Ib. Relation, Subgrouping, Order fixing

This is further divided into three sections viz.;.

1. Simple Relation;
2. Subgrouping;
3. Order Fixing

1. Simple Relation (sign :)

Examples :

1.	7 : 82	Art in relation to literature
2.	78 : 1	Music in relation to philosophy.
3.	791.43 : 316.3 or 316.3 : 791.43	Influence of Cinema on Society.

2. Subgrouping (sign [ ])

Examples

1.	0277.7 : [681.31 (540)] or 027.7 (540) : [681.31]	Computers in Academic Libraries in India.
2.	[63 + 626.84] (548.4)	Agriculture and irrigation in Andhra Pradesh

3. Order fixing (sign : :)

Examples

1.	061.2 (100) : : 002 FID	International Federation of Information and Documentation
2.	55 : : 54	Geo-chemistry

2.5.2. Subdivisions

The common auxiliary subdivisions consists of numerical tables in which common concepts are enumerated and listed hierarchically. These resemble like main tables but distinguished by their own symbols either prefixed or enclosing the main number. Some common auxiliaries such as Space and Time are relevant to any subject irrespective of its extension or intention. Other auxiliaries such as Form and Language become relevant as soon as a phenomena becomes the subject of the document. These common auxiliary subdivisions represent same concept with the some symbol or notation whatever may the place of their application in the schedules.

In order to distinguish or differentiate various types of common auxiliary groups found in UDC-IME-93, distinct symbols have been assigned to each of the groups. For example the digits 1 to 9 have several meanings in different contents in the schedules. But when these digits are enclosed in ( ) parenthesis it denotes 'Place'. Likewise = equal indicated Language, "....." quotation marks indicates Time and so on.

The common auxiliary subdivisions fall in to two groups : The independent and the dependent. These two groups are presented briefly in the subsections.

2.5.2.1. Independent Auxiliaries

These auxiliaries may be attached to any UDC class number where ever required and also can be used on their own to form the whole class number for a given title. These are present in table Ic to Ig - auxiliaries of languages, form, place, ethnic grouping and time.

2.5.2.2. Dependent Auxiliaries

These auxiliaries must always be attached to a UDC class number. These are present in tables Ii to Ik - auxiliaries of point of view, materials and persons. Table Ih - non-UDC notation is also dependent for all practical purposes as the symbols * asterisk and A/Z Roman capital letters have to be added to UDC class number.

Self Check Exercise - 2

1. In how many groups common auxiliary subdivision fall into.
2. What do you mean by independent common auxiliaries.
3. What symbols are used to indicate non UDC notation.

Note :

(a) Write your answers in the space given below :

(b) Compare your answer within the model answers given at the end of this unit.

....

....

....

....

....

2.6. INDEPENDENT AUXILIARY TABLES

As stated earlier the independent auxiliaries may be added to any UDC class number and also can be used on their own. Most of these tables have symbols that enclose the class number which distinguish it from adjacent number. These are 'biterminal signs' - the signs with both an opening and a closing element, is a starter and arrester. Tables Id, Ie and If i.e. Form, Place, Ethnic grouping have paranthesis. Table Ig - Time have quotation marks. Only Table Ic - Language has been assigned the symbol = equal sign. These auxiliaries with biterminal signs can be affixed at any part of UDC class number i.e. after beginning, middle or end i.e. prefixed, infixed or suffixed.

Examples

(540)	India. Republic of India
(540) 664.11	India. Cane Sugar Production
664(540).11	Production - India - Canesugar
664.11 (540)	Cane Sugar Production in India.

The independent common auxiliaries are presented briefly in the following subsections with worked out examples.

2.6.1. Common auxiliaries of language. Table Ic (P.2) Symbol = ... (equals)

These auxiliaries represent the language or linguistic form of a document whose subject matter or thought content is represented by main UDC number. These also form the basis for parallel divisions of 811 Languages and 821 Literatures of individual languages by substituting a point for = equal sign.

Examples

1. 027.6 (035) = 111 Hand book of special librarianship in English

2.	(051.555.2) = 572.24	Woman magazines in Telugu
3.	811.131.1	Italian Language.

Note : = 131.1 is taken from table Ic.

2.6.2. Common auxiliaries of form Table Id (P.15) Symbol (0 ...) brackets nought

These auxiliaries denote the form or presentation of documents and not used to denote the subject matter or thought content of the documents. Literary form are classed under 82-1/-9 at page 902 in the UDC schedules. These are generally used following a subject notation, but if desired can be used first followed by the subject notation.

Examples

1.	61(03)	Reference works on medicine
2.	33(051)	Periodicals on Economics
3.	(031) 66.0	Encyclopaedia of chemical engineering
4.	(540) (059)	Indian almanacs.

2.6.3. Common auxiliaries of place. Table Ie (P. 21). Symbol (1/9) brackets one to nine

These auxiliaries indicate the geographical range, locality or other spatial aspect of a subject or thought content of a document denoted by main UDC class number. These are also form the basis for the parallel division of 913/919 regional geography and 93/99 History by deleting the brackets and prefixing 91 or 9 respectively. These are normally used following subject notation. If necessary place auxiliary can be used first followed by the subject notation. These also may be interconnected in a UDC number so as to achieve a desired sequence.

Examples

1.	677(510)	Textile industry in China
2.	327 (540)	India's foreign policy
3.	339.13.012.42(73)	Free market in USA

or

(73)339.13.012.42

4. 354(410).32 British ministry of education

2.6.4. Common auxiliaries of ethnic grouping. Table If. (P. 65) Symbol (= ...) bracket equals

These auxiliaries denote nationality or ethnic aspects of a subject represented by main UDC class number. These are like table 5 : Racial and ethnic groups in Dewey Decimal Classification. These are derived from the common auxiliaries of language (Table Ic). In this table we also find political nationality denoted mainly by (=1.4/.9) which is derived from the common auxiliaries place (Table Ie). This common auxiliary normally follows the main UDC number.

Examples

1.	398.21(=72)	Fairy tales of Australian races.
2.	(=214.21)	Hindi speaking peoples.
3.	572.9(=081)	Ethnology of primitive races.

2.6.5. Common auxiliaries of time. Table Ig. (P. 66). Symbol "..." double quotation marks.

These auxiliaries denote the date, point of time or range of time of a subject represented by main UDC class number. The schedule is drawn on the basis of Christian Calender. The non-christian systems of time reckoning is provided at "68" and "69" i.e. secular time reckonings and non-christian religious time reckonings. Dates BC and AD may be identified by prefixing - to BC dates and + to AD dates. Dates are represented in the class number in the order of year - month - day enclosed in quotation marks. There is a provision in time auxiliaries to represent smaller time division such as : hour, minute or second when require in the construction of the class number.

Examples

1.	"1947.08.15"	15th August 1947

The non-significant places are to be represented by zeroes.

2.	"0556.07.01"	1st July AD 556.
3.	"1948.01.30.05.30.05	30th January 1948 at 5 hours 30 minutes, 5 seconds.

Self Check Exercise - 3

1. Which auxiliary tables in UDC have to be used in parenthesis.
2. What is meant by "bitermind signs".
3. List out independent common auxiliary tables.

Note :

(a) Write your answer in the space given below.

(b) Compare your answers with the model answers given at the end of this unit.

....

....

....

2.7. DEPENDENT AUXILIARY TABLES

These dependent auxiliary tables must be attached to UDC number. The tables Ii to Ik is auxiliary subdivisions such as point of view, materials and persons fall under this category. Table Ih is non UDC sources such as * asterisk and A/Z also fall under this category. The dependent auxiliaries are briefly presented in the following sections.

2.7.1. Common Auxiliaries Point of View. Table Ii (P. 73) Symbol .00 point nought

These auxiliaries denote the most general points of view which a subject may be considered. These include concept, theory, function, activity, processes, problems, production, installation etc. These are applicable throughout the scheme but especially in the main classes Sciences (5), Technology (6) and the Arts (7). These are not used independently or cited first in the compound class number. These can be used as suffixes to a main UDC class number.

Example

1.	303.03.001.5	Working hypothesis in Social Science Research.
2.	369.004.122	Advantages of social insurance
3.	821.572.24-13.000.141	Telugu epic poetry from philosophical point of view.

2.7.2. Common auxiliaries of materials Table Ik. (P. 76). Symbol - 03 hyphen nought three.

These auxiliaries denote the materials or constituents of which objects or products are made. These are applicable throughout the main tables if the material aspects is secondary to the subject. In classes such as 66 chemical technology and 67 various industries these auxiliaries are applicable most. These are not to be used independently or cited first in a compound class number. These are always suffixed to the main number or notation which expresses the subject to be qualified.

Examples

1.	746.7 - 035.26	Bamboo Basket Works
2.	746.3 - 037.3	Silk Embroidery
3.	684.457 - 035.3	Wooden Book Cases

2.7.3. Common Auxiliaries of Persons. Table Ik (P. 78). Symbol - 05 hyphen nought five.

These auxiliary divisions denote the persons concerned or their characteristics but not things or disciplines according to personal application. These are applicable throughout the scheme if the personal aspect is secondary to the main subject. These are not to used independently or cited first in a compound class number and are always suffixed to a main UDC class number which expresses the subject to be classified.

Examples

1.	33 - 05	Economists
2.	02 - 055.2	Women Librarians

3.	62 - 055.1	Male Engineers.

2.7.4. Subject specification by non-UDC sources. Table Ih (P. 73) Symbols * asterisk and A/Z

This table specifies means of adding non-UDC notation since the * asterisk and A/Z alphabetical extensions must be added to a main UDC number. This table is in two parts viz., 1. The asterisk and 2. direct alphabetical specification. The use of these two non-UDC notation is demonstrated in the following sub-sub-sections.

2.7.4.1. Asterisk

As stated already the asterisk * introduces a notation which is a non-UDC notation. The * asterisk may follow a UDC notation to introduce a word, symbol or number from a non-UDC source which is added in so as to specify a subject.

Examples

1.	656.224(540)*7008	Godavari Express (Train No. 7008).
2.	656.7 (540) * Ic - 927	Indian Airlines (Flight No. Ic-927)
3.	796.61 * Km 25	25 KM cycling

2.7.4.2. Alphabetical Specification

Alphabetical specification involves the use of proper names and acronyms direct to the main UDC base number. If this device is used in common auxiliaries of place (Table Ie) these alphabets A/Z be with the brackets.

Examples

1.	(548.1 - 2 Madurai)	Tamil Nadu - Madurai District.
2.	656.7 : 061.1 (540) IAC	Indian Airlines Corporation (IAC)
3.	929 Gandhi	Biography of Mahatma Gandhi.

Self Check Exercise - 4

1. Name the dependent auxiliary table in UDC.
2. Which table in UDC provides for subject specification by non-UDC sources.
3. For what purpose * asterisk is introduced in UDC.
4. For alphabetical specification in UDC which type of notation is used.

Note :

(a) Write your answers in the space given below :

(b) Compare your answers with the model answers given at the end of this unit.

....

....

....

....

2.8. SPECIAL AUXILIARY SUBDIVISIONS. SECTION II. (P. 83)

As the term denotes, special auxiliary subdivisions viz., 1/-9, .01/.09, '0/'9 are limited in their scope and application and each of the series is used to denote recurrent concepts in that part of the main schedule for which it is designated. Unlike common auxiliary signs and sub-divisions of Section 1, in the special auxiliaries the same notation may be used with different meanings in different places in the schedules. The use of the three types of special auxiliary subdivisions for synthesis or number building at different places in the schedules has been clearly stated with suitable worked out examples.

The three types of special auxiliary subdivisions is briefly presented in the following subsections.

2.8.1. Hyphen series -1/-9 (P. 83)

This series is analytical or differentiative in nature and indicate elements, components, properties and other details of the subject denoted by main UDC class number to which they apply. These are listed at different places in their schedules but especially at 62/69 and 82.

Examples

1.	62 - 5	Operation and control of machines and processes.
	621.181 - 5	Operation of steam boilers
2.	616 - 08	Treatment of diseases
	616.5 - 08	Treatment of skin diseases
3.	82 - 311.6	Historical novels
	821.214.21-311.6	Hindi historical novels

2.8.2. Point Nought Series .01/.09 (P. 83)

This series is more diversely used and developed in much more details than -1/-9. This series represent recurrent concepts such as aspect studies, activities, processes, operations, plant and equipment. These are listed at different places in the schedules especially under the classes 35, 71/79, 8 and 9.

Examples

1.	06.023.7	Honorary members of organisations
	061.12.023.7	Honorary members of academies.
2.	35.08	Officials (Public)
	354.53.08	Officials of Ministry of Health.
3.	76.023.1	Wood (graphic arts)
	762.1.023.1	Wood engraving

2.8.3. Apostrophe series '0/'9 (P. 83)

This series is more specific than the hyphen and point nought series. These are synthetic or integrative in nature representing compound subjects by compound notation. This series is profusely used in classes 329, 54, 669 and 82.

Examples

1.	329.11	Conservative parties
	329.18'11	Facist conservative parties

2.	547.46'052	Nitriles
	547.39'052	Nitriles acids
3.	81'37	Semantics.
	811.211'37	Sanskrit semantics

Self Check Exercise - 5

1. Describe special auxiliary divisions.
2. Name the three types of special auxiliaries employed in UDC.
3. List out three examples each in the schedules where three types of special auxiliaries have been employed.

Note :

(a) Write your answers in the space given below.

(b) Compare your answers to the model answers given at the end of this unit.

....

....

....

....

....

2.9. MAIN TABLES

As stated already main tables or the tern main classes are based on Dewey Decimal Classification. In UDC IME-93 the main class 4 is vacant as it was cancelled in 1963 to make room for further developments in the universe of the knowledge. The subject linguistics has been transferred to main class 8 literature in IME-85 and continued in IME-93.

In UDC-IME-93 we find the following (main) classes.

0 Generalities ...

1 Philosophy, Psychology

2 Religion, Theology

3 Social Sciences ...

4 (Vacant)

5 Mathematics and natural sciences

6 Applied sciences ....

7 The Arts ....

8 Language, Linguistics, Literature

9 Geography, Biography, History.

We can see that each of the above main class is represented by single digit - the Indo-Arabic numeral. This is analogous to the first summary of DDC. The three digit minimum as we find in DDC is not maintained in UDC. Each of the above ten classes (nine) is further divided to form ten narrower classes and the process continues to minutes divisions of a class.

2.9.1. Summary of Main Classes

In IME-93 Pages XIX to XXIV we find the summary of the main classes extended to second level classes (i.e. two digit numbers). Class 6 is summarised to three digit level. This is analogous the second summary i.e., 100 divisions in DDC. Certain numbers have been shown in [ ] square brackets which means that they are currently vacant.

The following is the summary of main tables (Schedules), for your familiarisation.

0	Generalities ...
00	Prolegomena ...
01	Bibliography ...
02	Librarianship
030	Encyclopaedias ...
050	Serial publications
06	Organisations ...
070	News papers, Journalism
08	Poly graphics....
09	Manuscripts ...
1	Philosophy, Psychology

11	Metaphysics
13	Philosophy of mind ...
14	Philosophical systems
159.9	Psychology
16	Logic ...
17	Moral philosophy, Ethics ...
2	Religion, Theology
21	Natural theology ...
22	The bible
23/28	Christianity
23	Dogmatic theology
24	Practical theology
25	Postoral theology
26	Christian Church ...
27	General history of Christian Church
28	Christian Churches ....
29	Non-christian religions
3	Social Sciences ...
30	Theories
31	Demography, Sociology.
32	Politics
33	Economics
34	Law
35	Public administration
36	Social work, Social aid ...
37	Education ...
389	Metrology ...
[4]	
5	Mathematics and natural sciences

51	Mathematics
52	Astronomy ...
53	Physics
54	Chemistry ...
55	Earth sciences ...
56	Paleontology
57	Biological sciences
58	Botany
59	Zoology
6	Applied sciences ...
61	Medical sciences
62	Engineering
63	Agriculture ...
64	Home economics ...
65	Management ...
66	Chemical technology...
67	Various industries ...
68	Industries, Crafts ...
69	Building trade ...
7	The Arts, Recreation, Sport....
71	Physical planning
72	Architecture
73	Plastic arts
74	Drawing ...
75	Painting
76	Graphic arts ...
77	Photography ...
78	Music
79	Recreation...

8	Language, Linguistics, Literature
80	General questions ...
81	Linguistics and languages
82	Literature
9	Geography, Biography, History.
91	Geography ...
929	Biographies and related studies
93/99	History
930	Science of history
931	Ancient history
94	Medieval and Modern history

The following numbers enclosed in [ ] square brackets are currently vacant in IME-93.

[03], [04], [05], [07], [12], [15], [18], [19], [38], [4], [50], [83|89], [90], [92], and [93].

2.9.2. Parallel divisions

The most important device introduced in the UDC-IME is Parallel divisions indicated by the symbol ≅ in the various parts of the schedules. This device indicates that the number preceding the ≅ may be subdivided in a manner analogous to the number following it. This device results in the same notation being used to denote a given concept in more than one place. This device is employed not only in the main schedules but also in common and special auxiliary tables. Here are few examples :

1. *Use in the schedules*

(a)	373.1	School organisation 373.1 ≅ 371
	373.1<u>3</u>	Teaching methods in school organisations (371.<u>3</u>)
(b)	611.3	Digestive system

611.3 ≅ 616.3

611.311.4 Floor of the mouth (616.311.4)

2. *Use in common auxiliaries*

(a) (081.2) Selected works

(0812.2) ≅ (082.2)

(081.2 2) Selected questions (082.22)

811.111(081.22) Selected quotations from English

(b) = 03 Translations

= 03.1/1.9 ≅ = 1/=9.

= 03.112.2 German translation = 112.2

54 = 03.112.2 Physics documents translated from German.

3. *Use in special auxiliaries*

(a) 616-002.2 Chronic inflammation

616 - 002.2 ≅ 616.002.1

616 - 002.216 Degenerative chronic inflammation (616.002.16)

611.3 - 002.216 degenerative chronic inflammation in digestive system

(b) 72.03 Schools, Styles, Influences

subdivisions ≅ 7.03

72.032.77 Ancient Roman Styles of Architecture

723.17.032.77 Architecture of Ancient Roman royal places. (7.032.77)

2.9.3. Intercalation

According to UDC intercalation means "the use of a auxiliary as an infix rather than a prefix or suffix". In other words, certain auxiliaries may interrupt a main UDC number creating a compound.

e.g. : 622.341 Ironore mining

622(594).341 Mining-Indonesia-Ironore

The reason for this type of intercalation is to achieve more helpful arrangement of documents. This may vary the agreed citation order in UDC to produce different sequences. If required common auxiliary of place can be brought before common auxiliary of time.

e.g. : 664.11 (729.1) "19" Sugar production, Cuba. 20th Century.

If required place auxiliary can still be brought further forward and intercalated in the main class number.

e.g. : 664(729.1).1119 Food production. Cuba. Cane sugar. 20th Century.

This type of intercalation can be resorted to if ones wish to group all documents on the subject 664 production and subdivide it by space before proceeding to ...11 cane sugar. If there is a need to group information about more specific activity such as production in a given area it can be done as follows :

664(729.1)	Food Production. Cuba
664.(729.1).11	Food Production. Cuba. Cane Sugar
664(729.1).12	Food Production. Cuba, Beat Sugar
664(729.2)	Food Production. Jamaica
664(729.2).11	Food Production. Jamaica Cane Sugar
664(729.2).12	Food Production. Jamaica. Beat Sugar and so on.

2.10. CITATION ORDER

Compound or complex subject requires various aspects or points of view to be represented in the class number. The order in which all these aspects and/or points of view have to be represented in the compound or complex class number is known as citation order. UDC-IME-93 defined citation order as "the order in which the elements are combined to make a compound number is the citation order" (P. XVI). The citation order is also known as facet formula.

In order to ensure a sequence from general to specific it is necessary that the filing order should be the reverse of the citation order. Conversely the citation order is the reverse of the filing order. This is simplest rule for citing elements in a compound or complex lass number. The elements in a compound/Complex class number proceed from special to general.

If one wish to cite say = 112.6 and (680) and "19" and .003.2 and .038 all qualifying 622.3421 the standard would be :

.038; .003.2, "19" (680) = 112.6, thus 622.3421.038.003.2 "19" (680) = 112.6

Gold mining-deposits-financial point of view - 20th century - South Africa - in Africans

Thus the standard citation prescribed in IME-93 is as follows :

Main No.	Special auxiliaries	View Point	Non-UDC notation
0/9	'1/'9, .01/.09, –1/–9	.001/.009	A/Z, *

Other Common auxiliaries

Time	Race & Nationality	Place	Form	Language
"..."	(= ...)	(1/9)	(0...)	=...

2.11. FILING ORDER

The prescribed filing order in UDC-IME-93 is from general to specific. As per the figure-2 for filing order prescribed at page XV is as follows :

Independent auxiliaries : =, (0...), (1/9), (=...) "..." followed by +, / simple number and followed by auxiliaries as suffixes, These are :

:, : :, = (0...), (1/9) (=...), "...", *, A/Z, .00, –0, – 1/–9, .0, ' - followed by next simple number. The above filing order is demonstrated in the following examples.

Symbol	*Example*
Independent Auxiliaries	
=	= 133.1 French language
(0...)	(0.035.5) Mimeographical documents
(1/9)	(44) France
(=...)	(=1.493) Belgians
"..."	"19" 20th Century
+	622.342 + 669.2 Gold oremining and non-ferrous metallurgy
/	622.343/349 Other ore mining
Simple number	622.342.1 Gold ore mining
Auxiliaries as suffixes	
:	622.342.1 : 338.123 Economic boom in gold ore mining
: :	622.342.1 : : 338.123 Economic boom in gold ore mining
=	622.342.1 = 133.1 Documents in French about gold ore mining
(0...)	622.342.1 (0.035.5) Mimeographic document on gold ore mining
(1/9)	622.342.1 (44) Gold ore mining in France
(=...)	622.342.1 (=1.493) Gold ore mining among Belgians
"..."	622.342.1"19" Gold ore mining in 20th Century
*	622.342.1 * 10 Gold ore mining in mine no. 20.
A/Z	622.342.1KOL Kolar Gold ore mining
.00	622.342.1.002.63 Raw products of gold ore mining
–0	622.342.1 – 057.162 Executives in Gold ore mining

–1/–9	622.342.1 – 781 Safety installation in gold ore mining
.0	622.342.1.031 Stratified character of gold ore deposits
	622.342.1 Intermediate products from gold ore mining

Next single number 622:345 Tin ores.

Self Check Exercise - 6

1. Find out class numbers for the following subjects from IME-93.
   - (a) Statistics
   - (b) Public Law
   - (c) Consumerism
   - (d) Italian Language
   - (e) Mechanics of gases
   - (f) Human Physiology
   - (g) chemical engineering
   - (h) Numismatics
   - (i) Essays (literature)
   - (j) Regional geography
2. Cite three examples of parallel division in UDC schedules.
3. What is meant by intercalation.
4. Define citation order.
5. Which auxiliaries come first in the filing order of UDC-IME-93.

Note :

(a) Write your answers in the space given below.

(b) Compare your answers to the model answers given at the end of this unit.

....

....

....

....

....

2.12. ALPHABETICAL SUBJECT INDEX

Part-2 of IME, English text, Edition 2 is Alphabetical subject index. It is intended to provide access to UDC classes set out in the schedule. It is not a substitute for the schedule, but enables fast access to UDC classes through the index terms arranged alphabetically. The index is arranged in word by word alphabetical order.

The index includes all principal divisions, common auxiliaries and special auxiliaries. It also includes qualifiers to be read in conjuction with the proceeding description. For example qualifiers such as : aviary, ornamental, paleozoology, Zoology, indicate context in which a term is used and where the said term is used in more than one context. This to achieve the user of the index to identify the correct alternative. For example :

birds

aviary	636.63
ornamental	636.68
Palaeozoology	568.2
Zoology	598.2

It also contains few cross references such as 'see also' and see'. The 'see also' cross reference is employed between related terms such as 'women' and 'female'. 'See' cross reference is employed to bring to the notice of the use of the index additional entries in the index. For example :

1. Anchoring devices

floating markers	627.714
gun mounting	623.435.6
manufacture	672.66

see also mooring facilities.

Here is an example from alphabetical subject index.

Painting

arts	75
buildings	698.1
ceramics	666.3.056

finished coats	667.653
furniture making	684.4.059
glass	666.1.058, 666.1.058.8
surface decoration	621.795.3

Self Check Exercise - 7

1. What type of material included in the alphabetical subject index.
2. Name the two types of cross references used in the index.
3. Cite few examples 'see also' cross referencing used in the index.
4. What is the purpose of alphabetical subject index.

Note :

(a) Write your answers in the space given below

(b) Compare your answers with the model answers given at the end of this unit.

....

....

....

....

2.13. SUMMARY

UDC is one of the most important general schemes of library classification. To meet the ever changing needs of user libraries and information centres UDC is being broughtout in the form of abridged and medium editions. The first international medium edition (IME) was published in 1985 and Part 2 : Alphabetical Subject Index in 1988. The second IME was Published in 1993 in two parts – Part 1 : Systematic tables and Part 2 : Alphabetical Subject Index.

In addition to various signs and symbols two more new symbols : → (arrow) meaning 'see also' and ≅ parallel division have been introduced in IME.

The provision of two kinds common auxiliaries viz. 1. sings

and 2. subdivision have greatly contributed to the synthetic nature of UDC.

The subdivisions have been broadly divided into : independent and dependent common auxiliaries. Independent auxiliaries constitute table Ic to Ig. Dependent auxiliary tables constitute table Ii, Ik and Ih. It also provides for three types of special auxiliary sub-divisions; hyphen series -1/-9, point nought series .01/.09, and apostrophe series '0/'9. The scope of the special auxiliaries is limited in nature and found in various places in the schedules.

The most important innovation introduced in IME is ≅ parallel divisions. The symbol indicates that the number proceeding the ≅ may be subdivided in a manner analogous to the number following it. This device has greatly contributed the number building process in UDC.

The addition of new common auxiliary tables Ik-03 materials and -05 persons is a significant feature of IME. Compound and complex subject requires various aspects and points of view to be represented in the class number. The order in which these aspects have to be represented in the class numbers is known as citation order. The filing order in UDC is from general to specific and it is the reverse order of citation order.

Part 2 of IME, English text, Edition is Alphabetical Subject Index. It is intended to provide access to UDC class as set out in the schedules. It is arranged in word by word alphabetical order. It includes all principal division, comma and special auxiliaries. It acts as a tool to the user for quick location of class number in the schedules of UDC.

2.14. ANSWERS TO SELF CHECK EXERCISES

Exercise - 1

1. Two parts. Part-1 : Systematic tables, Part-2 : Alphabetical subject index.
2. British Standards Institution (BSI), London.

3. 1. Common auxiliaries, 2. Special auxiliaries.

Exercise - 2

1. Two groups. Group 1 : Signs, Group 2 : Subdivisions
2. An independent auxiliary may be added to any UDC class number.
3. Two symbols : * asterisk and A/Z.

Exercise - 3

1. Auxiliary tables - Id (Form), Ii (Place) and If (Ethnic grouping and nationality)
2. The sign with both opening and closing element. Eg. ( ) Parenthesis.
3. Tables Ic, Id, Ie, If and Ig.

Exercise - 4

1. Table Ii point of view, Table Ik - 03 materials, and - 05 persons.
2. Table Ih.
3. To introduce a notation which is not an authorised UDC number
4. Letter notation A/Z.

Exercise - 5

1. Special auxiliary subdivisions are limited in their scope and application.
2. Hyphen series -1/-9, point nought series .01/.09, apostrophe series '0/'9.
3. (a) Hyphen series : 62, 66, 82
   (b) Point nought series : 0003, 22, 329
   (c) Apostrophe series : 81'0, 903'1, 547.46.

Exercise - 6

1. (a) 311 (b) 342
   (c) 366 (d) 811.12

(e) 533 (f) 612

(g) 66.0 (h) 737

(i) 82-4 (j) 913

2. (a) 294.31 (b) 341.61

   (c) 377.1

3. The use of an auxiliary as an infix rather than a prefix or suffix.
4. The order in which elements are combined to make compound number is known as citation order.
5. Independent auxiliaries.

Exercise - 7

1. All principal divisions, common auxiliaries and special auxiliaries.
2. 'See' and 'See also'.
3. Birth, Bridges.
4. To provide access to UDC classes set out in the schedules.

2.15. ASSIGNMENT

1. Find out on which page of UDC-IME-93, the layout of UDC entries is given.
2. Write a brief note on management of UDC.
3. From the main tables (schedules) given at page XIX, find out the class numbers for the following subjects.

   (a) Rare and remarkable books (b) Christian Church

   (c) Folklore (d) Micro biology

   (e) Civil engineering (f) Cinematography

   (g) Philology (h) Travel

4. What is the position of language auxiliary (Table Ic) in the citation of UDC class number.
5. How BC and AD dates are distinguished in UDC. (See Table Ig).

6. What is the scope of common auxiliaries of materials - 03 and persons -.05 (See Table Ik)
7. In how many ways special auxiliary subdivisions can be used in UDC (See Section II in UDC, Part-1).
8. Find out the class numbers for the following subjects with the help of systematic tables (Part-1) of UDC.

   (a) Free public libraries (b) Social ethics

   (c) Vedism (d) Science of economics

   (e) Telugu language (f) Fluid mechanics

   (g) Neuropathology (h) Sculpture

   (i) Physical geography
9. Find out the class numbers for the subjects with the help of Alphabetical Subject Index of UDC-IME-93.

   (a) Cost accounting (b) Liquid diet

   (c) English beef (d) First aid in mines

   (e) Children's hats (f) Processed milk

   (g) Oats Processing (h) Knowledge Phenomena

   (i) Sampling testing.

BLOCK 2 : PRACTICAL CLASSIFICATION WITH THE UDC

This block deals with the practical classification using UDC (IME-93). Unit 3 deals with the Common Auxiliary Tables found in the UDC for the construction of class numbers. These constitute signs and subdivision. Subdivision in turn are further divided into Independent and Dependent common auxiliary schedules. Unit 4 deals with Special Auxiliary Subdivisions which are found at several places in the tables of UDC. These are three types viz., Hyphen series, Point nought series and Apostrophe series and the three types appear both in the common auxiliaries and the main tables as well. Unit 5 deals with the syntheses or number building processing UDC. The synthesis is achieved with the use of common and special auxiliary subdivisions and parallel divisions which is an important synthetic device introduced for the first time in UDC (IME-1985). Unit 6 deals with the classification of titles falling under the main classes 0/9 and their divisions and subdivisions. The worked out examples covering the main classes and their divisions demonstrate the process of analysis and synthesis involved in classifying simple, compound and complex titles.

Unit 3
Common Auxiliary Tables

STRUCTURE

3.0. OBJECTIVES

The most innovative and influential features of UDC is its auxiliary tables which help for the construction of compound/ complex class numbers. After going through the unit you will be able to :

* Know the kinds of common auxiliaries provided in UDC.
* Understand the variety of independent common auxiliaries and apply them in the number building process.
* Grasp the variety of dependent common auxiliaries and use them for specifying various aspects in the compound class number; and
* Apply non-UDC notation for subject specification.

3.1. INTRODUCTION

In unit 2 you have been introduced to the salient features of international medium edition (IME-93). The most innovate feature of UDC is its auxiliary notation consisting of signs and subdivisions.

The common auxiliary signs include : the plus, the stroke, the colon, the square brackets and the double colon. The common auxiliary subdivisions consist of numeric tables. These fall in to two groups - the independent and the dependent. The independent auxiliaries constitute table Ic to Ig and the dependent are found at table Ii to Ik. In addition to these auxiliary table you will find table Ih which specifies means of adding non-UDC notation by the symbols * asterisk and A/Z Roman alphabets.

These common auxiliaries have been briefly presented in Unit-2. In this unit an attempt has been made to present the application of these common auxiliaries in the number building process or synthesis of a class number.

3.2. KINDS OF COMMON AUXILIARIES

The common auxiliaries in UDC comprise two kinds of symbols - the signs and subdivisions. The application of these two kinds is presented in the following sub-sections.

3.2.1. Signs

The common auxiliary signs constitute + the plus, / the stroke, : the colon, [ ] the square brackets and : : the double colon. In Section I of UDC at page 1 we find these signs.

3.2.1.1. Coordination . Extension +, /, (Table Ia) (P. 1)

Table Ia deals with + combination and / extension. This is further divided into two sections. Section 1 : Coordination and addition. Section 2 : Consecutive Extension.

Section 1. Coordination, Addition + (plus)

The coordination sign + plus connects two or more separated i.e., non-consecutive UDC numbers to denote a compound subject for which no single member is available in UDC.

Examples

1. Elements of Physics, Chemistry and Chemical Technology
   53 + 54 + 66
2. Agriculture in China and India
   63 (510 + 540)
3. Essence of Hinduism, Islam and Christianity
   294.11 + 297 + 23 / 28

Section 2 : Consecutive Extension / (stroke)

The extension sign / (stroke) connects the first and the last of the series of consecutive UDC number to denote a broad subject or range of concepts. This sign is very much used in the UDC schedules and we find several examples.

Examples

1. Introduction Christianity 23/28
2. Handbook of Ore deposits

   Analysis

   Ore deposits 553.3/.4

   Hand book (035) from table Id

Synthesis

553.3/.4 + (035) = 553.3/.4 (035)

3. Encyclopaedia of systematic physiology

Analysis

Systematic physiology	612.1/.8	
Encyclopaedia	(031)	from table Id

Synthesis

612.11.8 + (031) = 612.1/.8 (031)

4. Dictionary of applied arts in English

Analysis

Applied arts	745/749	
Dictionary	(038)	from table Id.
English language	= 111	from table Ic

Synthesis

745/749 + (038) + = 111 = 745/749 (038) = 111

3.2.1.2. Relation. Subgrouping. Order fixing :, [ ], : : (Table Ib). (P.1)

Table Ib deals with : relation, [ ] subgrouping and : : order fixing. This table is further divided into three sections : Section 1 : Simple Relation, Section 2 : Subgrouping and Section 3 : order fixing.

Section 1 : Simple Relation : (Colon)

The relation sign : (Colon) indicates relationship between two or more subjects connecting their UDC numbers. This is a dominant and very important sign by which we can indicate different types of relationship among the subjects.

Examples

1. Relationship between classification and cataloging

Analysis

Classification 025.4

Cataloging 025.3 (to be added with :)

Synthesis

025.4 + : 025.3 = 025.4 : 025.3

2. Comparative steady of religion and ethics

Analysis

Religion 2

Ethics 17 (to be added with :)

Synthesis

2 + : 17 = 2 : 17

3. Foreign policy of India towards Russia

Analysis

Foreign Policy 327

India (540) from table Ie

Russia (470)from table Ie (to be added with :)

Synthesis

327 + (540 + : 470) = 327 (540 : 470)

4. Influence climate on rice production

Analysis

Climate 504.38

Rice (Production) 633.18 (to be added with :)

Synthesis

504.38 + : 633.18 = 504.38 : 633.18 *or* 633.18 : 504.38

Section 2 : Subgrouping [ ] (Square brackets)

The symbol [ ] square brackets may be used as a subgrouping device within a complex combination of UDC numbers. This symbol is employed when a subject denoted by two or more UDC numbers is linked by plus sign, stroke or colon.

Example

1. Irrigation and rural engineering in India

Analysis

Irrigation	626.8	
Rural engineering	631.6	(to be added with +)
India	(540)	from table Ie

Synthesis

[626.8 + 631.6] + (540) = [626.8 + 631.6] (540)

2. International Council of Scientific Unions

Analysis

International organisations	061.1	
International	(100)	from table Ia
Science	5	to be added with :
International Council of Scientific Unions ICSU		(Alphabetical device)

Synthesis

061.1 + (100) + : [5] + ICSU = 061.1(100) : [5] ICSU

3. Banking services for social groups in rural settlements of Andhra Pradesh.

Analysis

Banking services	336.71	
Social groups	316.35	to be enclosed with [ ]
Rural Settlements	911.373	(to be added with :)
Andhra Pradesh	(548.4)	from table Ie

Synthesis

336.71 + [361.35 : 911.373] + (548.4) = 336.71 [361.35 : 911.373] (548.4)

4. Hindu musical works

Analysis

Musical works	78.02	
Hinduism	394	to be enclosed in [ ] and added with :

Synthesis

78.02 + : [294] = 78.02 : [294]

Section 3 : Order fixing. : : (Double Colon)

The symbol : : double colon may be used to fix the order of the component numbers in a compound number, especially when the UDC is used in a computer based mechanical information system. This is a new connecting sign introduced in IME.

Examples

1. United Nations Industrial Development Organisation (UNIDO)

Analysis

International organisation	061.1	
International	(100)	from table Ie
Industrial development	67	
United Nations Industrial Development Organisation	UNIDO (Alphabetical device)	

Synthesis

061.1 + (100) + : : + 67 + UNIDO
= 061.1(100) : : 67 UNIDO

2. Human Genetics.

Analysis

Human Physiology	612
Genetics	575

Synthesis

612 + : : 575 = 612 : : 575

3. War medicine

Analysis

War	355.01
Medicine	610

Synthesis

355.01 + : : 610 = 355.01 : : 610 or 610 : : 355.01

4. Photo Journalism

Analysis

Photography	77
Journalism	070

Synthesis

77 + : : 070 = 070 : : 77 or 77 : : 070.

Self Check Exercise - 1

1. How many kinds of common auxiliaries are found in UDC. Name Them.
2. Name the common auxiliary signs.
3. What are the signs used for coordination and extension.
4. What are the signs used for relation, sub-grouping and order fixing.

Note :

(a) Write your answers in the space given below:

(b) Compared your answers with the model answers given at the end of this unit.

....

....

....

....

....

....

3.2.2. Sub-divisions

The common auxiliary subdivisions consisting numeric tables in which concepts are enumerated and listed hierarchically. These look like main tables but distinguished by their own symbols either prefixed or enclosing the main number, The common auxiliary subdivisions fall into two groups viz., 1. the independent and 2. the dependent. These two groups are described briefly in the following sub-sub-sections.

3.2.2.1. Independent auxiliaries

As the term denotes these auxiliaries may be attached to any UDC class number wherever required. These also can be used on their own to form a whole class number for a given subject.

3.2.2.2. Dependent auxiliaries

As the term denotes these auxiliaries must always be attached to a UDC class number. The tables Ii to Ik is auxiliaries of point of view, materials and persons come under this category. Table Ih which specifies means of adding non-UDC notation is also comes under this category.

The worked out examples covering independent and dependent auxiliaries is presented in the following sections 3.3 and 3.4.

3.3. INDEPENDENT COMMON AUXILIARY TABLES

As stated earlier, the independent common auxiliary tables may be added to any UDC class number and also can be used on their own. Most of these tables have symbols which enclose a class number which distinguish them from the adjacent number. The symbols are called 'biterminal signs' i.e. the signs with the both opening and closing element. The tables Ic to Ig i.e. Language (Ic), Form (Id), Place (Ie), Ethnic grouping (If) and Time (Ig) come under this category. Worked out examples of each of these common auxiliary tables is presented in the following sub-sections.

3.3.1. Common Auxiliaries of Language. Table Ic. = ... equals (P.2)

The common auxiliaries of language represent the language or linguistic form of a document whose subject matter or thought content is denoted by a main UDC number. The auxiliaries are indicated by the sign = equals in the class number. In the citation order, the language auxiliary normally comes last. A brief note on the use of these auxiliaries is given at Page 2. You have been already introduced to this table in unit 2, section 2.6.1. The following are some more examples.

Examples

1. Encyclopaedia of library and Information Science in English

Analysis

Library and Information Science	02	
Encyclopaedia	(031)	from table Id
English language	= 111	from table Ic

Synthesis

02 + (031) + = 111 = 02 (031) = 111

2. Concise encyclopaedia of Islam in Urdu

Analysis

Islam	297	
Encyclopaedia	(031)	from table Id
Urdu Language	= 214.22	from table Ic

Synthesis

297 + (031) + = 214.22 = 297(031) = 214.22

3. C. P. Brown's English - Telugu dictionary

Analysis

Dictionary	(038)	
English language	= 111	from table Ic
Telugu language	= 572.24	from table Ic

Synthesis

(0.38) + = 111 + = 572.24 = (038) = 111 = 572.24

Note : As per the instructions under 81‘374 Lexicography at page 900 “dictionaries themselves are not classed here, but by the use of form auxiliary (038)”. Hence the above title was classed under (038).

4. India Today, a weekly journal in Hindi.

Analysis

Serial Publications	050	
Weekly (Publication)	"530.1"	from table Ig
Hindi	= 214.21	from table Ic

Synthesis

050 + "530.1" + = 214.21 = 050"530.1" = 214.21

5. Abridged editions of books for students

Analysis

Text book for students	(075)	from table Id
Abridged editions	(0.046.4)	from table Id

Note : Under (0.0...) at page 16 we find the instruction which states that a special auxiliary in Table Id can be used with a form auxiliary (01)/(09) by dropping initial digit 0 from the special auxiliary.

Synthesis

(075 + 0.046.4) = (075.046.4).

This compound auxiliary can be used to any specific subject.

6. Abridged editions of text books in Russian for student of Chemistry.

Analysis

Chemistry	54	
A bridged edition of text books for students	(075.046.4)	
Russian language	= 161.1	from table Ic

Synthesis

54 + (075.046.4) + = 161.1 = 54(075.046.4) = 161.1

7. Sivapuranam translated from Sanskrit into Kannada

Analysis

Siva Puranam (Sacred books) 294.118

Translated documents = 03 from table Ic

As per the instruction at = 03 (page 3) we have to denote the source language by = 03.1/.9 and the target language directly by =1/=9.

Sanskrit = 03.211

Kannada = 573.11

Synthesis

294.118 + = 03.211 + = 573.11 = 294.118 = 03.211 = 573.11

Self Check Exercise - 2

Assign class numbers to the following tables.

1. Multilingual glossaries in Medical Sciences.
2. Theses on biochemistry in French, German and Italian.
3. Guide book of silk textiles in Chinese.
4. Mahabhartam translated from Sanskrit into Telugu.
5. Research on Classical Tamil Language.
6. Telugu dialects of coastal Andhra Pradesh.

Note :

(a) Write your answers in the a space given below :

(b) Compare your answers with the model answers given at the end of this unit.

....

....

....

....

....

....

3.3.2. Common Auxiliaries of Form. Table Id. (0...) bracket nought (P.15)

The auxiliaries denote form or presentation of documents and are represented by the symbol brackets nought (0...). These are not used to denote the subject matter of the documents. Literary forms are not grouped under this table and listed at 82.1/.9. You have been already introduced to this table under unit 2 and section 2.6.2. The following are some more worked examples. This is one of the most frequently auxiliary tables in UDC.

1. Concise encyclopaedia of language and linguistics.

   Analysis

Language and linguistics	81	
Encyclopaedia	(031)	
Concise documents	(0.021.4)	from table Id

   Synthesis

   81 + (031 + 0.021.4) = 81(031.021.4)

   Note : At page 16 under (0.0...) physical features the following instructions is given. "Use as special auxiliaries with the form auxiliaries (01)/(09) or as (0.0...) when no particular form of document is concerned."

2. Miniature editions of paintings

   Analysis

Painting	75	
Miniature editions	(0.021.6)	from table Id

   Synthesis

   75 + (0.021.6) = 75(0.021.6)

3. *Indian Library Refresher*: a quarterly of Ess Ess Publications, New Delhi

   Analysis

Trade catalogues of publishers	017.4	
Ess Ess Publications	SSP(alphabetical device)	
Periodicals	(05)	from table Id.
Quarterly	"540.3"	from table Ig

   Synthesis

   017.4 + 558 + (05) + "540.3" = 017.4 = 558 (05) "540.3"

4. A dictionary of Kashmiri Proverbs and sayings.

Analysis

Provers	398.91	
Dictionary	(038)	from table Id.
Kashmiri	= 214.12	from table Ic.

Synthesis

398.91 + (038) + = 214.12 = 398.91 (038) = 214.12

Note : This title also can be grouped under 82-84.

5. Historical plays in Malayalam

Analysis

History	93/99	
Plays	(0 : 82 - 2)	as a form. from table Id.

Note : At page 15 under table Id we find that "Kinds of form not listed in table Id may be denoted by (0 : ...).

Malayalam	= 573.14	from table Ic

Synthesis

93/99 + (0 : 82 - 2) + = 573.14 = 93/99 (0 : 82.2) = 573.14

6. Guide books on tourism in India

Analysis

Guide books	(036)	from table Id
Tourism	379.85	
India	(540)	from table Ie

Synthesis

(036) + 379.85 + (540) = (036) 379.85 (540)

Note : As per the instruction at page 15 "all the documents of the same form or presentation may be grouped together under the appropriate form auxiliary. Hence the above example. If one wish to put under the subject, it is as follows:

379.85 (540) (036)

7. Women's magazine in Home Economics.

Analysis

Home economics	64	
Magazines	(051)	from table Id
Documents for women	(0.055.2)	from table Id
Women's magazines	(051 + 0.055.2)	

Synthesis

64 + (051 + 0.055.2) = 64(051.055.2)

8. Dictionary of systematic botany in Russian

Analysis

Systematic botany	582	
Dictionary	(038)	from table Id
Russian	= 161.1	from table Ic

Synthesis

(038) + 582 + = 161.1 = (038) 582 = 161.6

or 582(038) = 161.6

Self Check Exercise - 3

Assign class numbers for the following titles.

1. A collection of Telugu proverbs.
2. Encyclopaedia of ethics and logic.
3. Dictionary of Tibetan and English language
4. Hand book Silvi culture
5. Mounted atleses of human physiology.
6. 2006 New year's day greeting cards.

Note :

(a) Write your answers in the space given below.

(b) Compare your answers with the model answers given at the end of this unit.

....

....

....

....

....

3.3.3. Common Auxiliaries of Place. Table Ie. (1/9). Brackets one to nine. (P. 21)

The Common Auxiliaries of Place indicate the geographical range, locality or other spatial aspect of a subject denoted by a main UDC number. These are indicated by symbol (1/9) brackets one to nine. These also form the basis for the parallel divisions 913/919 'Regional geography' and 93/99 History by deleting the brackets and prefixing 91 or 9 respectively. These are generally used following a subject notation. The space auxiliaries also be intercalated by citing the place auxiliary first. You have been already introduced to this table in unit 2 section 2.6.3. This is one of the most important auxiliary table applicable to all classes and frequently used auxiliary table. The following are few more worked out examples.

Examples

1. National Income of Brazil.

Analysis

National income	330.56	
Brazil	(81)	from table Ie

Synthesis

330.5 + (81) = 330.5 (81)

2. Free trade between France and Germany.

Analysis

Free trade	339.5.012.42	
France	(44)	from table Ie
Germany	(430)	from table Ie to added with :

Synthesis

339.5.012.42 + (44 : 430) = 339.5.0124.42 (44 : 430)

or (44 : 430) 339.5.012.42

3. Indian military standards

Analysis

Military standards 355.15

India	(540)	from table Ie

Synthesis

355.15 + (540) = 355.15 (540)

Note : The place auxiliary can be intercalated as follows:

335 (540) . 15. Military affairs. India. Standards.

4. Geography of ancient Greece

Note : Under 913.2/.9 at page 909 Geography of ancient world we find the following parallel divisions

913.2/.9 ≅ (32/39)

Ancient Greece (37) from table Ie

Analysis

Geography of ancient world	913.2/.9
Ancient Greece	(3<u>7</u>)

Synthesis

913 + (3<u>7</u>) = 91<u>3.7</u>

5. Geography of modern Malaysia.

Note : 914/919 Geography of modern world

914/919 ≅ (4/9)

As per the above instruction for parallel division we have to take the number for Malaysia from table Ie.

Malaysia	(595)	from table Ie

Analysis

Geography of Asia	915
Malaysia	(<u>595</u>)

Synthesis

915 + (~~5~~<u>95</u>) = 915.<u>95</u>

6. Living standards of French North African states.

Analysis

Living standards 330.59

(1 = ...) place with reference to race (P = 1)

Details by (=...) table If.

As per the above direction

North Africa	(61)	from table Ie
French speaking peoples	(=133.1)	from table If

Synthesis

330.59 + (61 + = 133.1) = 330.59 (61 = 133.1)

7. Vocational training in rural areas of Andhra Pradesh.

Analysis

Vocational training	331.544	
Andhra Pradesh	(548.4)	from table Ie
Rural areas	(1 - 22)	

Note : (1 -2/ -4) Political units. Table Ie. The (-2 / -4) auxiliaries are applicable to (3/9). Hence, rural Andhra Pradesh (548.4 + 4 + -1 -22) = (548.4 - 22)

Synthesis

331.544 + (548 - 22) = 331.544(548 - 22).

8. Development of Cement Industry in SAARC Countries.

Analysis

Cement industry	669.94	
South Asia	(54)	from table Ie

Note : At page 23 under (1 - 6) grouping of states from various view points. - the auxiliaries under (1 - 6) can be used either in their general form or as special auxiliaries. Hence, (1 - 67) grouping of states according to economic - point of view.

SAARC countries (54 + 1 - 67 SAARC) = (54 - 67 SAARC)

Synthesis

669.94 + (54 - 67 SAARC) = 669.94 (54 - 67 SAARC)

9. Exploration to North polar circle

Analysis

Exploration	91	
Polar Circles	(160 - 26)	from table Ie
North	(1 - 17)	from table Ie

Synthesis

91 + (160 - 26 + 1 - 17) = 91(160 - 26 - 17)

10. Cargo shipping on river ganges

Analysis

River transport 656.62

Note : 656.621/.626 ≅ 656.611/.616

Cargo shipping	656.61<u>4.3</u>
Cargo shipping on river water ways	656.62<u>4.3</u>
River ganges	(282.253.21) from table Ie

Synthesis

656.624.3 + (282.253.21) = 656.624.3 (282.253.21)

Self Check Exercise - 4

Assign class number to the following titles.

1. Trade agreements between Iran and Bangladesh.
2. Polytechnic libraries in Urban areas of India
3. Arbitration treaies of boundaries between China and Russia.
4. Exploration of mountains with height of 4000 meters above sea level.
5. Guide books on world travel
6. Oils deposits in Bay of Bengal
7. Transport on Brahmaputra river system.
8. Annual meetings of British common wealth.

Note :

(a) Write your answers in the space given below.

(b) Compare your answers with the model answers given at the end of this unit.

....

....

....

....

....

....

....

....

3.3.4. Common Auxiliaries of Ethnic Grouping and Nationality. Table If. (= ...) Bracket equals (P. 65)

The common auxiliaries of ethnic grouping and nationality represent the nationality or ethnic aspects of a subject represented by main UDC class number. The symbol (=...) bracket equals denote these common auxiliaries in the class number. These are mainly based on the common auxiliaries of language (Table Ic). You have been already introduced to this table in unit 2, section 2.6.4. The following are worked out examples.

Examples

1. National festivals of Chinese

Analysis

National festivals 394.21

Chinese (= 581) from table Ig

Synthesis

394.21 + (= 581) = 394.21 (=581)

2. Psychology of North Americans.

Analysis

Psychology 159.9

Note : North Americans. (=1.4/.9) particular nationalities of the modern world (=1.4/.9) ≅ (4/9) (Table Ie). As per the above parallel division instruction we have to take member for North America from Table Ie.

North America (7)

North Americans (= 1.7)

Synthesis

159.9 + (=1.7) = 159.9 (=1.7)

3. Social life of telugu speaking people.

Analysis

Social life 316.7

Note : (=11/=8) linguistic - cultural groups.

(=11/=8) ≅ =11/=8 (Table Ic).

From the above parallel instruction we have to take telugu language from Table Ic.

Telugu language = 572.24 from table Ic

Telugu speaking people (=572.24)

Synthesis

316.7 + (=572.24) = 316.7 (=572.24)

4. Racial physiology of Negroes

Analysis

Racial physiology 572.79

Negroes (=414/=45) from table Ig

Synthesis

572.79 + (=414/=45) = 572.79 (=414/=45)

5. Demometrics of social demography of mountain dwellers of India.

Analysis

Social demography 314.145

Demometrics 314.018

Mountain dwellers	(=1.23)	from table If.
India	(540)	from table Ie

Synthesis

314.145 + ~~314~~.018 + (=1.23) = (540)

= 314.145.018 (= 1.23) (540)

6. Historical account of Voyages of Polynesians.

Analysis

Voyages	910.4	
Polynesians	(=622.82)	from table If
Historical account	(091)	from table Id

Synthesis

910.4 + (=622.82) = (091) = 910.4 (=622.82) (091)

Self Check Exercise - 5

Assign class number to the following titles.

1. Economic development of Indians in the USA.
2. Military life of ancient Romans.
3. Hand book of folk ballads of Jews.
4. Pre-historic settlements of African mountain dwellers.
5. Cultural history of ancient Egyptians.
6. Polygamy of North American Indians.

Note :

(a) Write your answers in the space given below.

(b) Compare your answers with the model answers given at the end of this unit.

....

....

....

....

....

....

3.3.5. Common Auxiliaries of Time. Table Ig "..." Double quotation marks (P. 66)

The common auxiliaries of time denote the date, point of time or range of time of a subject represented by the main UDC number. The symbol "..." double quotation marks indicate the time common auxiliaries in UDC class number. The table was drawn on the basis of Christian calender. But non-christian time reckoning were listed at "68" and "69". The time auxiliary is normally cited after the main UDC class number.

Dates are denoted by citing the ordinary calender notation in the order of year-month-day enclosed in quotation marks. BC and AD dates can be indicated by prefixing the - minus sign to dates BC and + plus sign to dates AD. Centuries and decades may be denoted by 2 and 3 digits. The range of time may be denoted by / stroke. You have been already introduced to time auxiliaries in unit 2, section 2.6.5. The following are some more worked out examples.

Examples

1. January 20th 2006, Indian Republic day celebrations.

Analysis

Republic	321.728	
Celebration	06.078	(to be added with :)
India	(540)	from table Ie
January 26, 2006	"2006.01.26"	from table Ig.

Synthesis

321.728 + :06.078 + (540) + "2006.01.26"

= 321.728 : 06.078 (540) "2006.01.26

Note : The non-significant places to be occupied by zeroes as per UDC guide lines at page 66.

2. Launching of space shuttle discovery on July 26, 2005 at 11 hours 25 minutes and 10 seconds from Kennedy Space Centre, Florida (USA).

Analysis

Space shuttle	629.782
Launching	629.075
Discovery	DIS (alphabetical device)
July 26, 2005 at 11 Hrs, 25 Min., 10 Sec.	"2005.07.26.11.25.10"

Synthesis

629.782 + 629.075 + DIS + "2005.07.26.11.25.10"
= 629.782.075 DIS "2005.07.26.11.25.10"

3. Alexander's invasions of India in 327 BC.

Analysis

Military campaigns	355.48	
India	(540)	from table Ie
327 BC.	"-0327"	from table Ig.

Synthesis

355.48 + (540) + "-0327" = 355.48(540) "-0327"

4. Social and political conditions of India during the Mughal rule. (1526 - 1717)

Analysis

Social and political conditions	308 : 32	
India	(540)	from table Ie
1526/1717	"1526/1717"	from table Ig

Synthesis

308 : 32 + (540) + "1526/1717"
= 308 : 32 (540) "1526/1717"

5. Gold coins of chalukyas of 3rd century AD found in Karanataka.

Analysis

Coins	737.1

Metals	-034	from table Ik
	-034 ≅ 669	

As per the above parallel division instruction we have to proceed to 669.

Gold	669.<u>21</u>	i.e. -0.34.<u>21</u>
3rd century	"02"	from table Ig
Karanataka	(548.2)	from table Ie

Synthesis

737.1 + - 0.34.21 + (548.2) + "02"

= 737.1 - 0.34.21 (548.2) "02"

6. IASLIC Bulletin, a quarterly journal

Analysis

Library and Information Science	02	
Journal	(05)	from table Id
Quarterly	"540.3"	from table Ig

Synthesis

02 + (05) + "540.3" = 02 (05) "540.3"

7. Skating in Himalayas during winter 2005.

Analysis

Skating	796.71	
Himalayas	(235.243)	from table Ie
2005	"2005"	from table Ig
Winter	"324"	from table Ig

Synthesis

726.71 + (235.243) + "2005" + "324"

= 726.71 (235.243) "2005" "324"

8. Hindu Lunar months

Analysis

Non Christian religions time reckonings 69 ≅ 29

"69" from table Ig.

As per the above parallel division instruction we have to proceed to 29.

Hindu-time reckoning	294 i.e., "69 + 294" = "694"	
Lunar Months	"3274"	from table Ig
		(To be added with :)

Synthesis

"694 + : 3274" = "694 : 3274"

The above time auxiliary can be applied to any UDC class number.

9. Fasting during Hindu lunar months.

Analysis

Fasting	392.82
Hindu lunar months	"694 : 3274"

Synthesis

392.82 + "694 : 3274" = 392.82 "694 : 3274"

Self Check Exercise - 6

Assign class number to the following titles.

1. Andhra pradesh formation day celebrations November 1, 2005.
2. University News : A weekly Journal of Higher Education.
3. History of modern Europe since 1789.
4. Summer Olympic games in Montreal Canada, in 1991.
5. India today 1975-2005 anniversary issue.
6. Air transport accidents in Iran during autumn 2005.

Note :

(a) Write your answers in the space given below.

(b) Compare your answers with the model answers given at the end of the unit.

....

....

....

....

....

....

3.4. DEPENDENT AUXILIARY TABLES

As the term indicates these auxiliaries must always be attached to a UDC number. These are listed at tables Ii to Ik i.e. the auxiliaries of point of view (table Ii), materials (table Ik - 03) and persons (table Ik - 05).

In addition the table Ih which specifies means of adding non-UDC notation is in practice are dependent auxiliaries. You have been already introduced to dependent auxiliaries in unit 2, section 2.7. The following sub-sections deals with workout examples of dependent auxiliaries.

3.4.1. Common Auxiliaries of Point of view. (Table Ii) (.00...) Point nought-nought. (P. 73)

These auxiliaries denote most general points of view from which a subject may be considered. These are applicable throughout the scheme especially in classes 5, 6 and 7. Excessive or unnecessary use of these auxiliaries must be avoided. These should be used when the expression of point of view facet is needed in the class number. These are always suffixed to the main UDC number.

Examples

1. The constitution of India from federal(ism) point of view.

Analysis

Constitutions	342.4	
India	(540)	from table Ie

Note : At page 74 under .000.1/.9 General approach. We find .000.0/.9 ≅ 0/9 from table Ii.

As per the above parallel divisions instruction we have to get number for federalism and add to .000

Federalism 323.172

Synthesis

342.4 + (540) + .000. + 323.172

= 342.4 (540) .000. 323.172

2. UDC-IME-1993, Practical point of view

Analysis

Decimal classification	025.45	
Universal Decimal Classification	UDC (alphabetical device)	
Practical point of view	.002	from table Ii

Synthesis

025.45 + UDC + .002 = 025.45 UDC .002

3. Progress of saving banks in India

Analysis

Savings banks	336.722	
India	(540)	from table Ie
Progress	.001.78	from table Ii

Synthesis

336.722 + .007.8 + (540) = 336.722 .007.8 (540)

4. Restoration of Leonardo Davinci paintings.

Analysis

Painting 75

Note : At page 866 under 75 we find that details of works of particular artist by alphabetial extension.

Leonardo Davinci	Davinci	(Alphabetical extension)
Restoration	.004.67	from table Ii

Synthesis

75 + Davinci + .004.67 = 75 Davinci .004.67

5. Soil testing rooms in rural area of Punjab.

Analysis

Soil 631.43

Testing rooms	.006.26	from table Ii
Punjab	545.2 PUN	from table Ie
Rural areas	(1 - 22)	from table Ie

Synthesis

631.43 + .006.26 + (545.2 PUN + 1 - 22)

= 631.43.006.26 (545.2 PUN - 22)

6. Administration in the Ministry of Railways.

Analysis

Ministry of Railways	354.41	
Administrative staff	.007.1	from table Ii

Synthesis

354.41 + .007.1 = 354.41.007.1

7. Membership of Indian Science Congress

Analysis

Science	5	
National Organisations	061.1	to be added with :
India	(540)	from table Ic
Membership	.008.8	from table Ii

Synthesis

5 + : 61.1 + .008.8 + (540) = 5 : 061 .1.008.8 (540)

8. Cooperative relations with customers in Jeweller industry.

Analysis

Jewelry (Industry)	671.12	
Relations with customers	.009.7	from table Ii

Under .009.7 we find the following parallel division instruction .009.7 ≅ .009.1

Cooperation .009.11

Synthesis

671.2 + .009.7 + 009.1<u>1</u> = 671.2 .009.7 <u>1</u>

9. Care of manuscripts in libraries of learned societies.

   Analysis

Libraries of learned societies	027.2	
Manuscripts	(0.032)	from table Id
Care	.004.53	

   Synthesis

   027.2 + .004.53 + (0.032) = 027.2.004.53 (0.032)

Self Check Exercise - 7

Assign class number to the following titles.

1. Output point of view of news print industry.
2. Modernisation point of minimizing enterprises.
3. Precision mechanisms in carpentry.
4. Mending point of view of industrial antiquities.
5. Archives Laboratories.
6. Furniture design experts.
7. Escalators as auxiliary equipment.
8. Advantages of mechanised economic production.

Note :

(a) Write your answers in the space given below.

(b) Compare your answers with the model answers given at the end of the unit.

....

....

....

....

....

....

....

....

....

3.4.2. Common Auxiliaries of Materials. Table Ik. - 03 Hyphen nought three. (P. 76)

These auxiliaries denote materials or constituents of which objects or products are made. The symbol -03 hyphen nought three indicates the common auxiliaries of materials in the class number. These are applicable throughout the main tables if the materials aspect is secondary to the subject. These are not to be used independently or cited first in a compound class number. These are always suffixed to the main UDC number. You have been already introduced to common auxiliaries of materials in unit 2, section 2.7.2.

The following are some more worked out examples for your familiarisation in the use of these auxiliaries.

Examples

1. Sapphires for Bracelets.

Analysis

Bracelets	671.121.3	
Precious stones	-032.8	from table Ik

Note : -032.81/.87 ≅ 553.81/.87

As per the above parallel division instruction we have to proceed to 553.81/.87

Sapphire 553.823 i.e., - 032.8 + 553.823 = Sapphire as material -032.823

Synthesis

671.121.3 + - 032.823 = 671.121.3 - 032.823.

2. Concrete for multistory buildings.

Analysis

Multistory buildings	69.036.8	
Concrete	= 033.3	from table Ik

Synthesis

69.036.8 + -033.3 = 69.036.8 - 033.8

3. Copper for camping equipment

   Analysis

   Camping equipment 685.53

   Copper - 034.3 from table Ik.

   Synthesis

   685.53 + - 0.34.3 = 685.53 - 034.3

4. Cotton fibre for lace making

   Analysis

   Lace making 746.21

   Cotton fibre -037.2 from table Ik

   Synthesis

   746.21 + 037.2 = 746.21 - 037.2

5. Synthetic fibres for women dresses.

   Analysis

   Women dresses 687.122

   Synthetic fibres -037.47

   Synthesis

   687.122 + -37.47 = 687.122 - 037.47

6. Proteins for biscuit production

   Analysis

   Biscuit production 664.81

   organic chemical and compounds -039.7 from table Ik

   -039.7 ≅ 547

   From the above parallel division instruction at page 78, we have to proceed to 547 and take the number for proteins.

   Proteins 547.<u>96</u> i.e., -039.796 = 664.81 - 039.796

   Synthesis

   664.81 + - 039.796 = 664.81 - 039.796

7. Tape for surgical dressing

Analysis

Surgical dressing 616-0.89.4

Tape -037.75 from table Ik

Synthesis

616 - 089.4 + - 037.5 = 616 - 089.4 - 037.5

8. Plant protein based plastic for dolls preparation.

Analysis

Dolls 688.721.2

Plastics -036.5 from table Ik

- 036.5 ≅ 678.5

From the above parallel division instruction, we have to proceed to 678.5 to get the number for plant protein.

Plant protein based plastics 678.562

i.e. -36.5 + 678.5<u>62</u> = - 036.5<u>62</u>

Synthesis

688.721.2 + - 036.562 = 688.721.2 - 036.562

Self Check Exercise - 8

Assign class numbers to the following titles.

1. Petroleum for motor cars.
2. Biumen for road laying.
3. Plaster of Paris for iconology.
4. Pulp for news print manufacturing.
5. Hair for wiggmaking industry.
6. Metal fibres for rope ways.
7. Mud for building bricks.
8. Hard wood for doors.

Note :

(a) Write your answers in the space given below.

(b) Compare your answers with the model answers given at the end of this unit.

....

....

....

....

....

....

....

....

3.4.3. Common Auxiliaries of Persons and Personal Characteristics. Table Ik. -05 Hyphen nought five (P. 78)

These auxiliaries denote the persons concerned or their characteristics, but not things or disciplines according to personal applications. The symbol - 05 hyphen nought five indicate persons in the UDC class number. These are applicable throughout the main tables if the personal aspect is second any to the subject. These are not to be used independently or cited first in a compound notation. These are to be suffixed to the main UDC number.

You have been already introduced to common auxiliaries of persons in unit 2, section 2.7.3. The following are some more worked out examples.

Examples

1. Biography of librarians

Analysis

Library science	02	
Persons	- 05	from table Ik
Biography	(092)	from table Id

Synthesis

02 + -05 + (092) = 02 - 05(092)

2. Living standards of mountain dwellers.

Analysis

Living standards 330.5

Mountain dwellers -054(23) from table Ik

Synthesis

330.5 + - 054(23) = 330.5 - 054 (23)

3. Teacher representatives

Analysis

Teaching 371.12

Persons as target - 052 from table Ik

Synthesis

371.12 + -052 = 371.12 - 052

4. Male teacher representatives

Analysis

Teachers representatives 371.12 - 052

Male persons - 055.1 from table Ik

Synthesis

371.12 - 052 - 055.1

Note : As per the guideline at page 78 under -05, we can use another common auxiliary of persons to the existing common auxiliary.

5. Old aged Cancer Patients

Analysis

Cancer 616 - 006.6

Patients - 052 from table Ik

Old aged persons - 053.9

Synthesis

616 - 006.6 + - 052 + - 053.9 = 616 - 006.6 - 052 - 053.9

6. Indian mathematical geniuses.

Analysis

Mathematics 51

Geniuses	-056.45	from table Ik
Indians	(= 1.540)	

Synthesis

51 + -056.45 + (=1.540) = 51 - 056.45 (=1.540)

7. Medical assistance to Tsunami Victims of Andhra Pradesh.

Analysis

Medial assistance	614.253.3	
Cyclones	551.466.6	(To be added with :)
Victims of disasters	- 058.66	from table Ik
Andhra Pradesh	(548.4)	from table Ie

Synthesis

614.253.3 + : 551.466.6 + - 058.66 (540)

= 614.253.3 : 551.466.6 - 058.66 (540)

8. International conference of cardiologists.

Analysis

Cardiology	612.17	
Persons	- 051	from table Ik
Conference	061.3	to be added with :
International	(100)	from table Ie

Synthesis

612.7 + -051 + : 061.3 + (100)

= 612.7 - 051 : 061.3 + (100) or 061.3 (100) : 612.7 - 051

9. Oldage Pensions to freedom fighters in Uttar Pradesh

Analysis

Oldage pensions	369/542	
Freedom fighters	- 058.566	from table Ik
Utter Pradesh	(545.8)	from table Ie

Synthesis

369.542 + - 058.566 + (545.8) = 369.542 - 058.566 (545.8)

10. Woman tennis players of India and China.

Analysis

Tennis	796.342	
Women	-055.2	from table Ik
India	(540)	from table Ie
China	(510)	(to be added with :)

Synthesis

796.342 + - 055.2 + (540 + : 510)

= 796.342 - 055.2 (540 : 510)

Self Check Exercise - 9

Assign class numbers to the following titles.

1. Hand book chemical engineers in USA.
2. Middle aged diabetes patients.
3. Hereditary rights to daughters.
4. Financial assistance to earth quake victims of Jammu and Kashmir.
5. Child film actors in Tamil.
6. Oldage male vocal musicians.

Note :

(a) Write your answers in the space given below.

(b) Compare your answer with the model answers given at the end of this unit.

....

....

....

....

....

3.4.4. Subject specification by Notations from Non-UDC Sources. Table Ih (P.73). Symbols * asterisk and A/Z.

This table specifies means of adding non-UDC notation since the symbols *asterisk and A/Z alphabetical extension must be added to the main UDC number. This table is in two parts. Part 1 : Asterisk and Part 2 : Direct Alphabetical specification. You have been already introduced to this Table in unit 2, section 2.7.4. The application or use of these two non-UDC notation is demonstrated in the following two sub-sections.

3.4.4.1. Asterisk (*)

This symbol * asterisk introduced a notation which is not an authorised UDC number. The asterisk may follow a UDC number to introduce a word, symbol or number from a non-UDC source to specify the subject concerned. The following are some more worked out examples.

Examples

1. Delhi Metro Rail route no. 10

Analysis

Underground railways	625.42	
Delhi	(545.5)	from table Ie
State Capital City	(1 - 25)	from table Ie
Delhi	DEL	(Alphabetical device)
Route No. 10	* 10	

Synthesis

625.42 + (545.5 - 1 - 25 + DEL) * 10

= 625.42 (545.5 -25 DEL) * 10

2. Indian National Satellite (INSAT) IC

Analysis

Artificial satellites	629.783
Indian National Satellite IC	* INSAT IC

Synthesis

629.783 + *INSAT IC = 629.783 * INSAT IC

3. Singarani Collaries mine no. 12

Analysis

Coal mining	622.333

Andhra Pradesh	(548.4)	from table Ie
Singarani calaries	SC	alphabetical device
Mine No. 12	* M. No. 12.	

Synthesis

622.333 + (548.4) + SC + * M. No. 12
= 622.333 (548.4) SC * M. No. 12.

4. Long distance 25 KMs. Walking

Analysis

Walking	796.51
25 KMs	* 25 KMs

Synthesis

796.51 + * 25 KMs = 796.51 * 25 KMs

5. Indian Airlines, Flight No. IC 927.

Analysis

Air travel	656.7	
India	(540)	from table Ie
Flight No. I 927	*IC 927	

Synthesis

656.7 + (540) + *IC 927 = 656.7 (540) *IC 927

3.4.4.2. Direct Alphabetical Specification A/Z

In UDC direct alphabetical specification involves the use of proper names or their abbreviations and acronyms. The letter notation A/Z may be added direct to the UDC base number with no asterisk or place intervening. The alphabetical specification of places from table Ie should be within parenthesis. You have already been introduced to alphabetical specification in unit 2, section 2.7.4.2. The following are some more worked out examples.

Examples

1. Bus services in Visakhapattnam City.

Analysis

Bus services 656.132

Visakhapattnam city (548.4 - 25 VIS) from table Ie

Synthesis

656.132 + (548.4 - 25 VIS) = 656.132 (548.4 - 25 VIS)

2. Hindustan Aeronautics Ltd.

Analysis

Aeronautical engineering 629.73

Govt. Organisation 061.1 to be added with :

India (540) from table Ie

Hindustan Aeronautics Ltd. HAL (alphabetical device)

Synthesis

629.73 + : 061.1 + HAL + (540)

= 629.73 : 061.1 HAL (540)

3. Works of Gurazada Appa Rao, famous Telugu Poet.

Analysis

Telugu Literature 821.572.24

Poetry 82-1

Gurazada Appa Rao Gurazada (alphabetical device)

Synthesis

821.572.24 + 82 - 1 + Gurazada

= 821.572.24 - 1 + Gurazada

4. Venkateshwara Hatcheries (Chicks)

Analysis

Hatchery 636.082.47

Venkateshwara Hatcheries VH (alphabetical device)

Synthesis

363.082.47 + VH = 363.082.47 VH

5. Biography of Mahatam Gandhi

Analysis

Biography 929

Mahatma Gandhi Gandhi (alphabetical device)

Synthesis

929 + Gandhi = 929 Gandhi

Self Check Exercise - 10

Assign class numbers to the following titles.

1. Osmania University, Hyderabad.
2. Track racing 250 KM
3. Doordarshan Kendra, Kolkata.
4. 60 Kg weight lifting.
5. Works of Rabindranath Tagore.
6. Annual Report of Oil and Natural Gas-Commission (ONGC), 2005.

Note :

(a) Write your answers in the space given below.

(b) Compare your answers with the model answers given at the end of the unit.

....

....

....

....

....

....

3.5. SUMMARY

The previous sections and sub-sections deal with common auxiliary tables employed in UDC. The variety of common auxiliary tables is most innovative and significant features of UDC. The common auxiliary tables are broadly divided into signs and sub-divisions. Further the sub-divisions are further divided into independent and dependent auxiliary tables. The signs employed in UDC include + / : [ ] : : . The independent common auxiliaries are listed at tables Ic to Ig. The dependent auxiliaries are listed at tables Ii to Ih.

The signs + and / are used for coordinating addition and consecutive extension respectively. The signs :, [ ], : : are used for relation, subgrouping and order fixing respectively.

The independent common auxiliary sub-divisions can be employed to any main UDC class number wherever appropriate. These also may be used on their own to form the whole class number fro a document. Most of these independent common auxiliary tables have symbols that enclose the number and thus demarcating ti from the adjacent numbers.

The dependent auxiliary tables must always be attached to a UDC number. These are listed at tables Ii to Ik i.e. the auxiliary tables of point of view, materials and persons. In addition, the table Ih specifies means of adding non-IDC notation. This includes * asterisk and A/Z alphabetial specification. This is in other words is known as subject specification by notations from non-UDC sources.

3.6. ANSWERS TO SELF CHECK EXERCISES

Exercise - 1

1. Two kinds : 1. Signs, 2. Sub-divisions
2. Plus, Stroke, Colon, Square brackets and double colon.
3. +, /
4. :, [ ], : :

Exercise-2

1. 61(038) = 00
2. 577 (043.2) = 133.1 = 112.2 = 131.1
3. 677.31 (036) = 581
4. 294.118 = 03.211 = 572.24
5. 811.573.15'02.001.5
6. 811.572.24'282 (548.4-210.5)

Exercise-3

1. 398.91(08) = 572.24
2. 16+17(031)
3. 811.548.6 + 811.111 or (038) = 584.6 = 111
4. 630 * 2(035)
5. 612(084.4.084.3 - 56)
6. 398.322.42 (089.7) "2006"

Exercise-4

1. 339.542.2 (55:549.3)
2. 027.7(540 - 21),
3. 346.631 (510 - 04 : 470 = 04)
4. 91(23 : 181 m 4000)
5. 910.4 (100) (038)
6. 553.98 (267.64)
7. 656.62 (282.253.22)
8. 061.1.06.053 (41 - 44)

Exercise-5

1. 330.34 (=1.540) (73)
2. 355.1 (=1.377)
3. 398.87 (=411.16) (035)
4. 903.4(=1.236)
5. 930.85(=1.32)
6. 314.545.4 (=81/=82)

Exercise-6

1. 321.013 : 06.078 (548.4) "2005.11.01"
2. 378(05) "530.1"
3. 940 "1789"
4. 796.032.2 (71-25 MON) "1991.322".
5. 050(540) "1975/2005"

6. 656.7.08 (55) “2005.323”

Exercise-7

1. 672.222.003.13
2. 622.012.001.76
3. 694.002.56
4. 904.6.004.67
5. 930.25.006.2
6. 684.4.007.62
7. 621.876.002.52
8. 338.363.004.122

Exercise-8

1. 629.331 - 032.32
2. 625.7 - 032.37
3. 73.04 - 033.21
4. 676.222 - 035.41
5. 687.512 - 035.55
6. 625.576.2 - 037.53
7. 666.712 - 032.6 ’22
8. 684.416 - 035.3

Exercise-9

1. 66 - 051 (73) (035)
2. 616.379 - 008.64 - 052
3. 347.65 - 055.62 - 055.2
4. 550.348.436 - 058.66 : 336
5. 791.071.2 - 053.5 = 573.15
6. 784 - 053.9 - 055.1

Exercise-10

1. 378.4 (548.4 - 25 HYD) OU
2. 796.72.093.52 * KM 250

3. 061.1 : 654.19 (541.23 - 25 KOL) DD
4. 796.88 * KG 60
5. 821.21 - 32 - 1 Tagore
6. 622.279 : 061.1 ONGC (540) (047) "2005"

3.7. ASSIGNMENT

Assign class number to the following titles.

1. Encyclopaedia of Religion and Ethics of Spanish.
2. The sports star, a weekly in English.
3. Miniature editions of Ajanta Paintings.
4. History of Library movement in Andhra Pradesh From 1900 to 1956.
5. Coalmining in Russia.
6. Foreign relations between Israel and Egypt.
7. Expeditions to mount Everest.
8. National festivals of Vietnamese.
9. Historical accounting of Voyages of Portuguese.
10. Freedom movement in India during the years 1857-1947.
11. Copper inscriptions of Rasthrakutas of 4th Century A.D. found in Maharastra.
12. Colon Classification 6th Edn. : Theoretical Point of View.
13. Development of urban cooperative banks in Tamil Nadu during 1990's.
14. Cement for building construction.
15. Diesel for rail transportation.
16. Biography of eminent chemical engineers of India.
17. Living standards of cave dwellers.
18. Air India flight no. 100.
19. Annual report of Osmania University, Hyderabad for the year 2005.
20. Works of Premchand an eminent hindi novelist.

Unit 4
Special Auxiliary Subdivisions

STRUCTURE

4.0. OBJECTIVES

The provision of special auxiliaries in the tables (schedules) and common auxiliaries has greatly contributed to synthesis or number building process in the UDC. After going through this unit you will be able to :

* Understand the nature and characteristics of special auxiliary subdivisions ;
* Know the three types of special auxiliaries and their application in number building ;
* Apply the three types of special auxiliary subdivisions each singly or in combination with one another; and
* Find out the occurrence of special auxiliaries in the common auxiliaries and main tables (schedules) as well and apply these in the number building process.

4.1. INTRODUCTION

In unit 2, section 2.8 you have been briefly introduced to the provision of special auxiliary subdivisions in UDC-IME-1993.

In section II of IME-93 (Page 83), we will find the provision of the three types of special auxiliary subdivisions viz.; 1. hyphen series (-1/-9), point nought series (.01/.09) and apostrophe series ('0/'9). The application of these three types of special auxiliaries is briefly presented in section II at Page 83, with suitable examples. The use of these special auxiliaries in number building process and their occurrence in the common auxiliaries and main tables (schedules) is presented to you in the succeeding sections and subsections.

4.2. NATURE AND CHARACTERS OF SPECIAL AUXILIARY SUBDIVISIONS

As the term 'special' denotes that the special auxiliaries are not listed at one place and the applicability is restricted. These occur at various places in the tables and common auxiliaries to certain extent. These can be applied only when indicated and the same notation may be used elsewhere with a different meaning. These can not be used independently unlike independent common auxiliaries, and should be used as suffixes to main UDC class numbers.

Generally these are listed immediately under a main number where they are valid. If there is no specific instruction, they are applicable also to all the direct divisions of that number. For example :

Under 37 Education, Teaching ... (page 232) we will find the provision of special auxiliary subdivisions ranging 37.0/37.08. There is no instruction as to their applicability. Therefore these special auxiliaries can be used to 37/379 and their subdivisions.

Example

37.011	Basic Concepts
378	Higher Education
378.011	Basic concepts in higher education

At certain places in the tables we will find the use or applicability of special auxiliaries is either restricted or extended from this norm. The range of applicability is indicated by a note. For example under 35 public administration we will find the provision of special auxiliaries with the following note "the .07/.08 special auxiliaries listed here are also applicable in the other divisions of class 3, as indicated at 3.07 and 3.08" (page 207).

Example

35.072.1	Centralization
311.21	Statistical research
311.21.072.1	Centralisation of statistical research.

We will also find the provision of special auxiliaries within other series of common auxiliaries. For example at the beginning table Ie, Common auxiliaries of place we find the occurrence of special auxiliary subdivisions (P. 21). These can be used in the form in which they appear. The note under special auxiliary subdivisions (1 - 0/-9) Boundaries .... states that "the (-0/-9) special auxiliaries may be combined with the (2/9) common auxiliaries to denote specific parts of geographic concepts. They also may be used with (1) with a general significance". (P. 21).

Example

(1 - 21)	Municipalities
(540)	India
(540 - 21)	Municipalities in India.

The above compound common auxiliary number can be attached to any main UDC number.

Example

Sanitary inspection and control in municipalities in India

Analysis

Sanitary inspection and control	614.3
Municipalities in India	(540 - 21)from table Ie

Synthesis

614.3 + (540 - 21) = 614.3 (540 - 21)

Some times we also find a special auxiliary within other special auxiliaries. For example at 78.06 various questions concerning music.

For subdivisions, see 7.06 ...

Example of Combination.

Utility aspect of music

78.06 + 7.06<u>7.4</u> = 78.06<u>7.4</u>

Note : As per the direction under 78.06 we have to proceed to 7.06 and take number for utility aspect. The number for utility aspect is 7.067.4.

Self Check Exercise - 1

1. In how many ways special auxiliaries are listed. Cite them.
2. Give two examples of listing special auxiliaries under common auxiliary sub divisions.
3. What are the characteristics of special auxiliaries.

Note :

(a) Write your answers in the space given below.

(b) Compare your answers with the model answers given at the end of this unit.

....

....

....

....

....

....

4.3. TYPES OF SPECIAL AUXILIARY SUBDIVISIONS

The section II of UDC (P. 83) deals with special auxiliary subdivisions. Three kinds of notation are used as special auxiliary subdivisions.. These are : 1. the hyphen series -1/-9, 2. the point nought series .01/.09, the apostrophe series '0/'9. The point nought series is most frequently used series in the IME-93. The following subsections deal with the three types of special auxiliary subdivisions with suitable worked out examples.

4.3.1. The Hyphen Series (-1/-9)

This series is mainly analytical or differentiative in functions, serving to denote elements, components, properties and other details of the subject denoted by main UDC class number to which these are to be applied. Mostly the application of this type is found in the main classes 5 Sciences, 6 Technologies and 82 Literature. The following are worked out examples.

1. Molten state of crystalline solids

   Analysis

Crystalline solids	544.22
Molten state	54 - 143

   Synthesis

   544.22 + ~~54~~ - 143 = 544.22 - 143

2. Surgical treatment of hepatitis

   Analysis

Hepatitis	616.36 - 002
Surgical treatment	616 - 089.8

   Synthesis

   616.36 - 002 + ~~616~~ - 089.8 = 616.36 - 002 - 089.8

3. Programme control and regulation of steam turbines.

   Analysis

Steam turbines	621.165
Programme control and regulation	62 - 503.55

   Synthesis

   621.165 − ~~62~~ - 503.55 = 621.165 - 503.55

4. Operation and control of sewing machines

   Analysis

Sewing machines	631.331
Operation and control	62 - 51

   Synthesis

   631.331 + ~~62~~ - 51 = 631.331 - 51

5. Natural cooling of food stuffs

   Analysis

Food stuffs	641.1

Note : Under 64 Home economics we find the following note. "The -1 - 9 auxiliaries from 62 - 1/- 8 and 66 - 9 are applicable throughout 64" (P. 641). Hence we have to proceed to 62 for getting number for natural cooling.

Natural cooling 62 - 71

Synthesis

641.1 + 62 - 71 = 641.1 - 71

6. Soap granules

Analysis

Soap industry 661.187

Note : Denote state and shape of soap-4 ... (from 62.4 ...). As per this note we have to proceed 62.4 ... for getting number for granules.

Granules 62 - 492.3

Synthesis

661.187 + 62 - 492.3 = 661.187 - 492.3

7. Solidified state of natural rubber

Analysis

Natural rubber 678.4

Note : Under 678 - 2/- 9 we find the following instruction. "The special auxiliaries -2 / -9 from 62 - 2/ - 8 and 66 - 9 are applicable throughout 678". Hence we have to proceed to 62 - 2 / -8 to get number for solidified state".

Solidified state 62 - 405

Synthesis

678.4 + 62 - 405 = 678.4 - 405

8. Reinforced concrete processes

Analysis

Reinforced concrete 691.328

Note : Under 69 Building (P. 835) we find the following instruction. " The -1 / -9 auxiliaries from 62 - 1 / - 8 and

66 - 9 are applicable through out 69". Hence we have to proceed to 69 to get number for processes.

Processes 66 - 932

Synthesis

691.328 + 66 - 932 = 691.328 - 932

9. Fantasy films in Chinese language.

Analysis

Films 791.43

Note : Under 791.43 (P. 883) we find the following instruction. "The -1 / -9 auxiliaries from 82 - 1/ - 9 are applicable to 791.43". Hence we have to proceed to 82 - 1 / - 9.

Fantasy (plays) 82 - 252

Chinese language = 581 from table Ic

Synthesis

791.43 + 82 - 252 + = 581 = 791.43 - 252 = 581

10. Marathi historical novels.

Analysis

Individual literature 821

Note : Under 821 (P. 905) we find the following note. "The sub division of 821 can be derived from =1 / =9 (Table Ic Languages) by substituting a point for the equal sign".

Marathi language = 214.35 from table Ic

Historical novels 82 - 311.6

Synthesis

821 + = 214.35 + 82 - 311.6 = 821.214.35 - 311.6

11. Rotation of Pluto

Analysis

Pluto 523.482

Rotation 52 - 327

Synthesis

523.482 + ~~52~~ - 327 = 523.482 - 327

12. Crystalline state of organic matter.

Analysis

Organic matter	543.38
Crystalline state	54 - 162

Synthesis

543.38 + ~~54~~ - 162 = 543.38 - 162

4.3.2. The Point-nought Series (.01/.09)

These special auxiliary subdivisions are more diversely used and developed in much more detail than -1 / -9. These represent sets and subsets of recurrent concepts such as aspect studies, activities, processes, operations, plants and equipment. The point-nought series of special auxiliary subdivisions are found at many places in the schedules. The following are worked out examples.

1. Uses and styles of picture writing

Analysis

Picture writing	003.21
Uses and styles of writing	003.07

Synthesis

003.21 + ~~003~~.07 = 003.21.07

2. Group investigation of psychophysiology.

Analysis

Psychophysiology	159.91
Group investigation	159.9072.43

Synthesis

159.91 + ~~159~~.9072.43 = 159.91.072.43

3. Versions of New Testament.

Analysis

New Testament	225

Versions 22.014

Synthesis

225.22.014 = 225.014

4. Sovereignty in Parliamentary democracy

Analysis

Parliamentary democracy 321.72

Sovereignty 321.011

Synthesis

321.71 + ~~321~~.011 = 321.71.011

5. Compulsory secondary school education.

Analysis

Secondary school education 373.5

Compulsory schooling 37.014.14

Synthesis

373.5 + ~~37~~.014.14 = 343.5.014.14

6. Television techniques in practical cartography.

Analysis

Practical cartography 528.92

Television techniques 528.8041.8

Synthesis

528.92 + ~~528.8~~.041.8 = 528.92.041.8

7. Climatic effects on plant reproduction.

Analysis

Plant reproduction 581.16

Climatic effects 58.056

Synthesis

581.16 + ~~58~~.056 = 581.16.056

8. Tissue structure of central nervous system

Analysis

Central nervous system 611.018

Tissue structure 611.018

Synthesis

611.81 + ~~611~~.018 = 611.81.018

9. Management of Police dogs.

Analysis

Police dogs 636.74

Management 636.083.1

Synthesis

636.74 + ~~636~~.083.1 = 636.74.083.1

10. Mechanisation of Hotel industry.

Analysis

Hotel industry 640.4

Mechanisation 64.011.54

Synthesis

640.4 + ~~64~~.011.54 = 640.4.011.54

11. Surrealism in painting

Analysis

Painting schools and styles 75.03

Surrealism 7.037.5

Synthesis

75.03 + ~~7~~.037.5 = 75.03 7.5

12. Speed capacity of cycling

Analysis

Cycling 796.1

Speed capacity 796.012.13

Synthesis

796.1 + ~~796~~.012.13 = 796.1.012.13

4.3.3. The Apostrophe Series ('0/'9}

This special auxiliary subdivisions unlike -1/-9 and .01/

.09 is often synthetic or integrative in function denoting compound subjects by compound notation. These are listed at few places in the schedules especially at 546 and 82. At other places these are derived from the main numbers by parallel division. At page 321 under 546 in organic chemistry the use of apostrophe is indicated with the following instruction that "the chemical compound is denoted by means of the apostrophe. The following are worked out examples.

1. Nationalist republican attitude.

   Analysis

   Nationalist attitude 329.17

   Note : At page 149 under 329.1/.6 classification of political parties we find the following instruction "for parties and movements with several political aims, the apostrophe '... may be used to combine the subdivisions of 329".

   Republican attitude 329.23

   Synthesis

   329.17 + ~~329~~.23 = 329.17'.23

2. Sodium nitrate

   Analysis

   Sodium Na 546.33

   Nitrites 546.173

   Synthesis

   546.33 + ~~546~~.173 = 546.33'173

3. Alloys of copper, nickel and zinc

   Analysis

   Copper alloys 669.35

   Nickel 669.245

   Zinc 669.5

   Synthesis

   669.35 + ~~669~~.245 + ~~669~~.5 = 669.35'.245'.5

4. Regulating water supply sources.

   Analysis

Water supply sources	628.11
Regulating	628.1'181

   Synthesis

   628.11 + 628.1'181 = 628.11'181

5. Practical knowledge of Russian language.

   Analysis

   Languages 811

   At page 901 under 811 we find the following note.

   Note : "The subdivision of 811 can be derived from =1/=0 (Table Ic language) by substituting a point for the equal sign.

Russian	= 161.1	from table Ic
Practical knowledge	81'24	

   Synthesis

   811 + = 161.1 + 81'24 = 811.161'24

6. Weapons of nomadic cultures

   Analysis

Weapons	903.22
Nomadic Cultures	903'15

   Synthesis

   903.22 + 903'15 = 903.22'15

7. Acid methanol esters

   Analysis

   Acids 547.29

   Note : Under 547.29 (at page 327) we find the following instruction. "Denote esters by apostrophe combination with subdivisions of 547.26".

   Methanol 547.261

Synthesis

547.29 + ~~547.26~~1 = 547.29'1

8. Alloys of gold and silver

Analysis

Gold alloys	669.215
Silver	669.22

Synthesis

669.215 + ~~669.~~22 = 669.215'22

9. Alloys of zinc and lead

Analysis

Zinc alloys	669.15
Lead	669.4

Synthesis

669.15 + ~~669.~~4 = 669.15'4

10. Dogmatist, fascist, anarchist parties.

Analysis

Dogmatist party	329.147
Fascist party	329.18
Anarchist party	329.285

Synthesis

329.147 + ~~329.~~18 + ~~329.~~285 = 329.147 '18 '285

Self Check Exercise - 2

Assign Class Numbers to the following titles.

1. Endoscopy of cardiac complaints
2. Kashmiri love songs
3. Nonemperical of sowing and planting machines
4. Nonemperical research in Monogamy.
5. Pedagogue guidance in elementary education.
6. Construction of astrometric instruments
7. Silicon Borides

8. Yak Milk
9. Dictionary of homonyms in telugu
10. Idioms in French

Note :

(a) Write your answers in the space given below.

(b) Compare your answers with the model answers given at the end of this unit.

....

....

....

....

....

....

....

....

....

4.4. APPLICATION OF SPECIAL AUXILIARY SUBDIVISIONS

In the preceding section 4.3 you have been introduced to the application of the three types of special auxiliaries viz. -1/-9, .01/.09, '0/'9 in the number building process. The worked out examples have amply demonstrated the role of these special auxiliary subdivisions in enhancing the synthetic nature of UDC. These three types an be used either singly or in combination with other auxiliaries. The following subsections deal with use of these auxiliaries at three levels i.e., 1. citing a single auxiliary, 2. citing several auxiliaries with a the same symbol and 3. citing several auxiliaries with different symbols.

4.4.1. Citing a single auxiliary

The three types of special auxiliary subdivisions viz., -1/-9, .01/.09, '9/'9 can be used singly in the number building process. The following are worked out examples.

1. Telugu crime novels

   Analysis

   Telugu literature 821.572.24

   Crime novels 82 - 312.4

   Synthesis

   821.572.24 + ~~82~~ - 312.4 = 821.572.24 - 312.4

2. Shape and form of lignine base plastics.

   Analysis

   Lignine base plastics 678.557

   Shape and form 678 - 4

   Synthesis

   678.557 + ~~678~~ - 4 = 678.557 - 4

3. Physical methods of grafting of plant.

   Analysis

   Grafting 631.541

   Physical method 631.53.027.3

   Synthesis

   631.541 + ~~631.53~~.027.3 = 631.541.027.3

4. Reformation of Criminal law

   Analysis

   Criminal law 343

   Reformation 34.04

   Synthesis

   343 + ~~34~~.04 = 343.04

5. Potassium cyanate

   Analysis

   Potassium 546.32

   Cyanate 546.268.1

   Synthesis

   546.32 + ~~546~~.268.1 = 546.32'268.1

6. Grammar of Sanskrit

Analysis

Sanskrit language	811.211
Grammar	81‘36

Synthesis

811.211 + ~~81~~‘36 = 811.211‘36

4.4.2. Citing Several Auxiliaries with the Same Symbol

Each one type of special auxiliary subdivision can be cited in a class number by using the same connecting symbol. That means each type of special auxiliary subdivision can be used more than once if required, for building a class number. The result of this process is a homogeneous chain. The following are worked out examples.

1. Surgical treatment of throat caner

Analysis

Throat	616.321
Tumors	616-006

Synthesis

616.321 + ~~616~~ - 006 + ~~616~~ - 089 = 616.321 - 006 - 089

2. Malayalam comedy and tragedy plays.

Analysis

Malayalam literature	821.573.14
Tragedies	82 - 21
Comedies	82 - 22

Synthesis

821.573.14 + ~~82~~ - 21 + ~~82~~ - 22 = 821.573.14 - 21 - 22

3. Reference and loan services in public libraries.

Analysis

Public libraries	027.4
Reference service	027.081

Loan service	027.082

Synthesis

027.4 + ~~027~~.087 + ~~027~~.082 = 027.4.087.082

4. Technical questions relating to manuscript writing

Analysis

Manuscripts	091.2
Technical questions	091.0
Writing	091.01

Synthesis

091.2 + ~~091~~.0 + ~~091~~.01 = 091.2.0.01

5. Alloys of tin, copper and zinc

Analysis

Tin alloys	669.65
Copper	669.3
Zinc	669.5

Synthesis

669.65 + ~~669~~.3 + ~~669~~.5 = 669.65'3'5

6. Grammar of classical Sanskrit

Analysis

Sanskrit language	811.211
Classical	81'02
Grammar	81'36

Synthesis

811.211 + ~~81~~ + '02 + ~~81~~'36 = 811.211'02'36

4.4.3. Citing Several Auxiliaries with Different Symbols

At page 83 under section B and subsection C we find the use of several special auxiliaries with different symbols which leads to a heterogeneous chain. There is no specific mention as to the sequence of the three types of special auxiliary subdivisions in the class number. The apostrophe series '0/'9 are usually more specific than –1/–9 and .01/.09. In the worked out examples at page 83 under subsection (C), we find the sequence of use of these three types as : '0/'9, -1/-9 and .01/.09. The following are worked out examples.

1. Communist-socialist left parties.

   Analysis

Communist parties	329.15
Socialist parties	329.14
Left parties	329.054.4

   Synthesis

   329.15 + 329 . 14 + 329 . 054.4 = 329.15'14.054.4

2. Methane lactide structures.

   Analysis

Methane	547.211
Lactides	547 - 313
Structures	547.022

   Synthesis

   547.211 + 547 - 313 + 547 .022 =547.211 - 313.022

3. Trends in Bengali lyric poetry

   Analysis

Bengali literature	821.214.32
Lyric poetry	82 - 14
Trends	82.02

   Synthesis

   821.214.32 + 82 - 14 + 82.02 = 821.214.32 - 14.02

4. Crude shapes and form remains of Metalartefacts of nomadic cultures.

   Analysis

Pre history	903
Nomadic cultures	903'15

Metalartefacts	903.05
Crude shapes and forms	903 - 4

Note : 903 - 4 ≅ 62 - 4

Crude	62 - 412
Crude shape and form	62 - 4 + 62 - 412 = 62 - 412

Synthesis

903 + ~~903~~'15 + ~~62~~ - 412 + ~~903~~.05 = 903'15 - 412.05

Note : In the above worked out examples all the three types of special auxiliary subdivisions is used.

5. Surrealistic historical films

Analysis

Films	791.43
Historical films	791.43 - 24
Surrealistic style	791.43.037.5

Synthesis

791.43 + ~~791.43~~ - 24 + ~~791.43~~.037.5 = 791.43 - 24.037.5

6. Benedictine religions orders and vows.

Analysis

Benedictines	271.1
Vows	271 - 3
Religious orders	271.02

Synthesis

271.1 + ~~271~~ - 3 + ~~271~~.02 = 271.1 - 3 02

7. Functional methods of applied socio-linguistics.

Analysis

Linguistics	81
Applied sociolinguistics	81'272
Functional method	81 - 116.3

Synthesis

81 + ~~81~~'272 + ~~81~~ - 116.3 = 81'272 - 116.3

8. Expertise in improvement of villages

   Analysis

   Villages (Physical planning) 711.437

   Note : Under 711 - 1 General principles and practice 711 - 1 ≅ 711.1

   Improvement 711.163 i.e., 711 - 16 3

   Expertise 7.072

   Synthesis

   711.437 + ~~711~~ - 163 + ~~7~~.072 = 711.437 - 163 .072

Self Check Exercise - 3

Assign class numbers to the following titles.

1. Citation order in UDC.
2. Activities and exhibitions of Academies.
3. Jewish interpretation of old testament.
4. Japanese short stories
5. Forms and shapes of wild silk
6. Diagnosis and treatment of asthma
7. Potassium aluminium
8. Telugu phonetics
9. Asymmetric and symmetric phenyls
10. Fantasy film styles

Note :

(a) Write your answers in the space given below.

(b) Compare your answers with the model answers given at the end of this unit.

....

....

....

....

....

....

4.5. OCCURRENCE OF SPECIAL AUXILIARIES IN COMMON AUXILIARIES

In the proceeding section 4.4 you have been introduced to the application of special auxiliary subdivisions by citing singly or citing several with the some symbol and or citing several auxiliaries with different symbols with worked out examples. In the following subsections you will be introduced to the occurrence of special auxiliary subdivisions in some of the common auxiliary subdivisions found in section I of UDC (P.1).

These special auxiliaries found in common auxiliaries may be used in the form in which they appear. For example at the beginning of table Id : Common auxiliaries of form we find the listing of special auxiliary subdivisions (P. 16). For example : (0.027.2) Standard editions. The special auxiliary element beginning with (.0) may be detached and affixed to any other direct division of (0...).

Eg. : Encyclopaedias (031)

Standard editions (0.027.2)

Standard editions of encyclopaedias

(031 + Ø.027.2) = (031.027.2)

The above compound number thus formed is still a common auxiliary which may be added to any UDC class number.

Eg. : Standard editions of chemical technology Encyclopaedias.

Analysis

Chemical technology 66

Standard editions of encyclopaedias (031.027.2)

Synthesis

66 + (031.027.2) = 66(031.027.2)

In the following subsections you will be introduced to the occurrence of special auxiliary subdivisions in the tables Id : Common auxiliaries of form, Ie : Common auxiliaries of place and If : Common auxiliaries of ethnic grouping and nationality with suitable worked out examples.

4.5.1. Common auxiliaries of form. Table Id (P. 15)

If you peruse the common auxiliaries of form you will find the occurrence of special auxiliary subdivisions at the beginning of table Id (P. 16) of IME-93. The range of these special auxiliaries is (0.02/0.08). Again you will find the occurrence of special auxiliary subdivisions under (084.3) (P. 19). The range of these subdivisions is (084.3 - 1 / 084.3 - 56). The following worked out examples will provide you an idea as to the application of special auxiliaries along with common auxiliaries of form.

Examples

1. Popular editions of hand books on chemistry.

Analysis

Chemistry	54
Hand books	(035)
Popular editions	(0.027.3)

Synthesis

54 + (035 + Ø.027.3) = 54(035.027.3)

2. Micro copies of dissertations on economics.

Analysis

Economics	33
Dissertations	(043.3)
Microcopies	(0.035.2)

Synthesis

33 + (043.3 + Ø.035.2) = 33(043.3.035.2)

3. Mounted atlases of human physiology

Analysis

Human physiology	612
Atlases	(084.4)
Mounted	(084.3 - 56)

Synthesis

612 + (084.4 + Ø84.3̸ - 56) = 612 (084.4 - 56)

4. Rolled wall maps on Indian hydrology.

Analysis

Hydrology	556	
India	(540)	from table Ie
Wall maps	(084.35)	
Rolled	(084.3 - 52)	

Synthesis

556 + (540) + (084.35 + Ø84.3̸ - 52)

= 556(540)(084.35 - 52)

5. Women's weekly magazines on home economics.

Analysis

Home economics	64.05	
Periodicals	(05)	
Documents for women	(0.055.2)	
Weekly	"530.1"	from table Ig

Synthesis

64.05 + (05 + Ø.055.2) – "530.1"

= 64.05 (05.055.2) + "530.1"

4.5.2. Common auxiliaries of place. Table Ie (P. 21)

The common auxiliaries of place table Ie (P. 21) provides for special auxiliary subdivisions at the beginning of the table. The range of these special auxiliaries is (1 - 0/-9). Again you will find the provision of special auxiliary subdivisions at the following places in the schedules. These are : (23) i.e. (23.0 / 23.075), (26) i.e., (26.02 / 26.07), (282) i.e. (282.03 / 282.05). As per the note at page 21, "the (-0/-9) special auxiliaries may be combined with (2/9) common auxiliaries to denote specific parts of geographic concepts. They may also be used with (1), with a general significance.

Examples

1. Prevention and control of communicable disease in urban areas of Uttar Pradesh.

Analysis

Prevention and control of communicable diseases 614.4

Uttar Pradesh	(545.8)
Urban areas	(1 - 21)

Synthesis

614.4 + (545.8 + 1 - 21) = 614.4(545.8 - 21)

2. Road transport in northwestern India

Analysis

Road transport	656.1
India	(540)
North West	(1 - 16)

Synthesis

656.1 (540 + 1 - 16) = 656.1 (540 - 16)

3. Hunting sport in tree zones of Himalayas.

Analysis

Hunting (sport)	799.2
Himalayas	(235.243)
Tree zones	(23.071)

Synthesis

799.2 + (235.243 + 23.071) = 799.2(235.243.071)

4. Passenger shipping through sea canals of Atlantic Ocean.

Analysis

Passenger shipping	656.614.2
Atlantic Ocean	(261)
Sea Canals	(26.06)

Synthesis

656.614.2 + (261 + .06) = 656.614 (261.06)

5. Reservoir on the lower course of river Godavari.

Analysis

Reservoir	627.81
Rivers of Indian subcontinent	(282.253.2)
Godavari	Godavari (alphabetical device)
Lower course	(282.044)

Synthesis

627.81 + (282.253.2 Godavari + 282.044)

= 627.81 (282.253.2 Godavari .044)

6. Tourism in ASEAN countries.

Analysis

Tourism	379.85
South East Asia	(59)
Countries according to economic point of view	(1 - 67)
ASEAN	= ASEAN (alphabetical device)

Synthesis

379.85 + (59 + ~~1~~ - 67 + ASEAN) = 379.85 (59 - 67 ASEAN)

4.5.3. Common Auxiliaries of Ethnic Grouping and Nationality. Table If (P. 65)

We find special auxiliary subdivisions under (= 088) mixed race and these are four in number. The following worked out examples indicate the use of these special auxiliary subdivisions.

Examples

1. Self determination movement of Colonial peoples of Latin America.

Analysis

Self-determination	323.17

Latin Americans (= 1.8)

Colonial people (= 1 - 5)

Synthesis

323.17 + (= 1.8 + = 1 - 5) = 323.17 (= 1.8 - 5)

2. Social structure of aboriginal races of Africa

Analysis

Social structure	316.3
Africans	(= 1.6)
Aboriginal races	(= 1 - 81)

Synthesis

316.3 + (= 1.6 + = 1 - 81) = 316.3 (= 1.6 - 81)

3. Material assistance to native Peruvians.

Analysis

Material assistance	364.42
Peruvians	(= 1.85)
Natives	(= 1 - 82)

Synthesis

364.42 + (= 1.85 + = 1 - 82) = 364.42(= 1.85 - 82)

4. Social psychology of naturalised Arabs

Analysis

Social psychology	316.6
Arabs	(= 411.21)
Naturalised	(= 1 - 86)

Synthesis

316.6 + (= 411.21 + = 1 - 86) = 316.6 (= 411.21 - 86)

Self Check Exercise - 4

Assign class numbers to the following titles.

1. Preprints of Periodicals on Genetics.
2. Flat wall maps of tropical cyclones.
3. Industrial production in under developed countries of Africa.

4. Mountaineering on snow zones of European mountains.
5. Oil deposits in Godavari river course.
6. Marriage customs native Chinese.

Note :

(a) Write your answers in the space given below.

(b) Compare your answers with the model answers given at the end of this unit.

....

....

....

....

....

....

....

....

4.6. OCCURRENCE OF SPECIAL AUXILIARIES IN THE MAIN TABLES (SCHEDULES)

If you observe the tables (schedules) of UDC-IME-93, you will notice the occurrence of special auxiliary subdivisions at various places. You will find the provision of three kinds of special auxiliary subdivisions at the beginning of a main class or at the beginning of a divisions of a main class. The provision of these auxiliary subdivisions is indicated by bold face. These subdivisions are followed by principal divisions of that main class or its subdivisions.

Of the tree types of special auxiliary subdivisions, you will find that point nought series .01/.09 occur frequently throughout the tables followed hyphen series -1/-9 and lastly by apostrophe series '1/'9. In the following subsections the provision or occurrence of the three types of special auxiliary subdivisions in different main classes is presented with worked out examples.

4.6.1. Generalities 0

This main class includes branches of knowledge such as :00 Prolegomena, 01 Bibliography, 02 Librarianship, 050 Serial Publications, 06 Organisations, 070 News Papers, Journalism, 08 Polygraphies and 09 Manuscripts. For some of these branches, you will find the provision of special auxiliary subdivisions followed by principal divisions.

Examples

1. Emergence of hieroglyphs

Analysis

Hieroglyphs	003.212
Emergence	003.02

Synthesis

003.212 + ~~003~~.02 = 003.212.02

2. Authority of Indian Standards

Analysis

Indian Standards	006.35 (540)IS
Authority	006.03

Synthesis

006.35(540) IS + ~~006~~.03 = 006.35(540) IS.03

3. Accession Catalogues of Private Libraries.

Analysis

Catalogues of Private Libraries	017.2
Accession Catalogues	017.092

Synthesis

017.2 + ~~017~~.092 = 017.2.092

4. Practical application of thesauro facet.

Analysis

Thesauro facet	025.48
Practical application	025.4.02

Synthesis

025.48 + ~~025.4~~.02 = 025.48.02

5. Research in private museums

Analysis

Research in museums	069.8
Private museums	069.017

Synthesis

069.8 + ~~069~~.017 = 069.8.017

6. Writing of paper manuscripts.

Analysis

Paper manuscripts	091.2
Writing	091.01

Synthesis

091.2 + ~~091~~.01 = 091.2.01

4.6.2. Philosophy. Psychology 1

This main class includes important subjects such as : 11 Metaphysics, 13 Philosophy of mind, 14 Philosophical systems, 159.9 Psychology, 16 Logic and 17 Moral philosophy. For some of these subjects we will find the provision of special auxiliary subdivisions.

Examples

1. Physiological theories of sex psychology.

Analysis

Sex psychology	159.922.1
Physiological theories	159.9.016.6

Synthesis

159.922 + ~~159.9~~.016.6 = 159.922.1.016.6

2. Biological theories of abnormal psychology.

Analysis

Abnormal psychology	159.97

Biological theories 159.9.015.7

Synthesis

159.97 + 159.9.015.7 = 159.97.015.7

3. Principles of epistemology.

Analysis

Epistemology 165

Principles 164.041

Synthesis

165 + 164.041 = 165.041

4. Moral facts of social ethics

Analysis

Social ethics 172

Moral facts 17.02

Synthesis

172 + 17.02 = 172.02

4.6.3. Religion. Theology 2

This main class includes branches of religion such as : 21 Natural theology, 22 The Bible, 23/28 Christianity, 24 Practical theology, 25 Pastoral theology, 26 Christian Church, 27 General history of Christian Church, 28 Christian Churches, and 29 Non-Christian religions. For some of these branches we find the provision of special auxiliary subdivisions.

Examples

1. Verbal concordances of Gospels.

Analysis

Gospels 226

Verbal concordances 22.031

Synthesis

226 + 22.031 = 226.031

2. Ritual books of African sects.

   Analysis

   African sects 264.014.5

   Ritual books 264 - 15

   Synthesis

   264.014.5 + 264 - 15 = 264.014.5 - 15

3. Jesuits missions

   Analysis

   Jesuits 271.5

   Missions 271 - 9

   Synthesis

   271.5 + 271 - 9 = 271.5 - 9

4. Matters of conscience of moral virtues

   Analysis

   Moral virtues 241.53

   Matters of conscience 241.1

   Synthesis

   241.53 + 241.01 = 241.53.01

5. Recipient of the sacraments by the communion.

   Analysis

   Communion 265.32

   Recipients of the sacraments 265.018

   Synthesis

   265.32 + 265.018 = 265.32.018

4.6.4. Social sciences 3

The main class 3 Social sciences include branches such as : 30 theories, 31 Demography, 32 Politics, 33 Economics, 35 Public and ministration, 36 Social work, 37 Education and 39 Ethnology. In most of these branches we find the occurrence of .01/.09 point nought series of special auxiliary subdivisions. The following worked out examples will demonstrate the application of special auxiliary subdivisions.

Examples

1. Structured sample size

Analysis

Sample size	303.522
Structured	303.042

Synthesis

303.522 + ~~303~~.042 = 303.522.042

2. Cooperation in planned social development.

Analysis

Planned social development	613.43
Cooperation	316.4.063.34

Synthesis

316.43 + ~~316.4~~.063.34 = 316.43.063.34

3. Opposition Republican Parties.

Analysis

Republican Parties	329.23
Opposition	329.052

Synthesis

329.23 + ~~329~~.052 = 329.23.052

4. Decentralization of cooperative companies.

Analysis

Cooperative companies	334.73
Decentralization	334.012.74

Synthesis

334.73 + ~~334~~.012.74 = 334.73.012.74

5. Codification of International Criminal Law

Analysis

International Criminal Law	341.4

Codification 641.018

Synthesis

341.4 + 341.018 = 341.4.018

6. Formation of local authorities

Analysis

Local authorities 352

Formation 35.074

Synthesis

352 + 35.074 = 352.074

7. State contributions to health insurance.

Analysis

Health insurance 369.22

State contribution 369.041

Synthesis

369.22 + 369.041 = 369.22.041

8. Refresher courses on adult education

Analysis

Adult education 374.7

Refresher courses 37.018.46

Synthesis

374.7 + 37.018.46 = 374.7.018.46

9. Origin of philately

Analysis

Collecting as hobby 37.9.824

Origin 379.8.091

Philately 656.835.91 (to be added with :)

Synthesis

379.824 + 379.8.091 + : 656.835.9

= 379.824.091 : 656.835.9

10. Extent of assistance to community works

    Analysis

    Community works 364.46

    Extent of assistance 364.017

    Synthesis

    364.46 + ~~364~~.017 = 364.46.017

4.6.5. Mathematics and Natural Sciences 5

The main class mathematics and natural sciences include important subject fields such as : 51 mathematics, 52 Astronomy, 53 Physics, 54 Chemistry, 55 Earth Sciences, 56 Palaeontology, 57 Biological sciences, 58 Botany and 59 Zoology. In all these subject fields we will find the occurrence .01/.09 point nought series of special auxiliary subdivisions. The following are worked out examples covering the application of special auxiliaries.

Examples

1. Five figure of mathematical tables.

    Analysis

    Mathematical tables 519.66

    Five figure tables 519.66.095

    Synthesis

    519.66 + ~~519.66~~.095 = 519.66.095

2. Magnetic field of stars.

    Analysis

    Stars 524.3

    Magnetic field 52 - 337

    Synthesis

    524.3 + ~~52~~ - 337 = 524.3 - 337

3. Landing of helicopters (Aerodynamics)

    Analysis

    Helicopters 533.661

Landing 533.6.015.2

Synthesis

533.661 + ~~533.6~~.015.2 = 533.661.015.2

4. Analytical procedure of organic matter

Analysis

Organic matter 543.38

Analytical procedure 543.06

Synthesis

543.38 + ~~543~~.06 = 543.38.06

5. Commercial reserves of manganese deposits.

Analysis

Manganese deposits 553.31

Commercial reserves 553.045

Synthesis

553.3 + ~~553~~.045 = 553.3.045

6. Fossilization of mamalia

Analysis

Mamalia 569

Fossilization 56.012

Synthesis

569 + ~~56~~.012 = 569.012

7. Metabolism of plankton

Analysis

Plankton 574.583

Metabolism 57.017.7

Synthesis

574.583 + ~~57~~.017.7 = 574.583.017.7

8. Climatic effects on flowers.

Analysis

Flowers 581.48

Climatic effects 58.056

Synthesis

581.48 + 58.056 = 581.48.056

9. Change of function of Nervous system in Animals.

Analysis

Nervous system (animals) 591.48

Change of function 591.4.068.1

Synthesis

591.48 + 591.4.068.1 = 591.48.068.1

10. Field observation of Bird Sanctuaries.

Analysis

Special animal reserves 502.742

Field observation 502.051

Birds 598.2 (to be added with :)

Synthesis

502.742 + 502.051 + :598.2 = 502.742.051:598.2

4.6.6. Applied Sciences. Medicine. Technology 6

This main class include subject areas such as : 61 Medical sciences, 62 Engineering, 63 Agriculture, 64 Home economics, 65 Management, 66 Chemical technology, 67 Various industries, 68 Industries and 69 Building (Construction) trade. In the schedules for these important branches of applied sciences we find the occurrence of -1/-9 hyphen and '1/'9 apostrophe series of special auxiliary subdivisions frequently and thus contribute the synthesis or number building process in UDC-IME-93. The following are typical worked out examples covering various branches of applied sciences.

Examples

1. Surgical treatment of glaucoma

Analysis

Glaucoma 617.7.007.681

Surgery 616 - 089

Synthesis

617.7 - 007.681 + ~~616~~ - 089 = 617.7 - 007.681 - 089

2. Servo control of power supply system.

Analysis

Power supply systems 621.311

Servo control 62 - 503.59

Synthesis

621.311 + ~~62~~ - 503.54 = 621.311 - 503.54

3. Prevention and control of injuries to racing horses.

Analysis

Racing horses 636.12

Prevention and controlling injuries636.093

Synthesis

636.12 + ~~636~~.093 = 636.12.093

4. Human resources for restaurants.

Analysis

Restaurants 640.432

Human resources 64.011.34

Synthesis

640.432 + ~~64~~.011.34 = 640.432.011.34

5. Economic objectives of printing industry

Analysis

Printing industry 655.1

Economic objectives 65.011.12

Synthesis

655.1 + ~~65~~.011.12 = 655.1.011.12

6. Storage and preservation of spiced breads.

Analysis

Spiced breads 664.667

Storage and Preservation 664.66.03

Synthesis

664.667 + ~~664.66~~.03 = 664.667.66.03

7. Manufacturing process of ear jewellry.

Analysis

Ear jewellry 671.121.4

Manufacturing process 67.02

Synthesis

670.121.4 + ~~67~~.02 = 671.121.4.02

8. Real-time operation in automatic digital computers.

Analysis

Automatic digital computers 681.322.2

Real-time operation 681.3.014

Synthesis

681.322.2 + ~~681.3~~.014 = 681.322.2.014

9. Maintenance of air-conditioning units

Analysis

Air-conditioning units 697.94

Maintenance 69.059.1

Synthesis

697.94 + ~~69~~.059.1 = 697.94.059.1

10. Emergency treatments of pregnant women

Analysis

Pregnant women 618.2

Emergency treatment 616.083.98

Synthesis

618.2 + ~~616~~.083.98 = 618.2.083.98

4.6.7. The Arts, Recreation, Sport 7

This main class consists of subjects such as : 71 Physical

planning, 72 Architecture, 73 Plastic arts, 74 Drawing, 75 Painting, 76 Graphic arts, 77 Photography, 78 Music and 79 Recreation. We find the use of special auxiliary point nought series .01/.09 in most of these subject fields. The following worked out examples demonstrate the use of special auxiliary subdivisions.

Examples

1. Ancient roman town planning.

   Analysis

Tour planning	711.4
Ancient Roman style	7.032.77

   Synthesis

   711.4 + ~~7~~.032.77 = 711.4.032.77

2. High rise bank buildings

   Analysis

Bank buildings	725.24
High rise buildings	72.011.27

   Synthesis

   725.24 + ~~72~~.011.27 = 725.24.011.27

3. Modern bronze artistic works.

   Analysis

Bronze artistic works	739.5
Modern art	7.06"189"

   Synthesis

   739.5 + ~~7~~.036"189" = 739.5.036"189"

4. Popular artistic wood works

   Analysis

Artistic wood works	745.51
Popular art	7.067.26

   Synthesis

   745.51 + ~~7~~.067.26 = 745.51.067.26

5. Painting of self portraits.

   Analysis

Painting	75
Self portraits	7.041.53

   Synthesis

   75 + ~~7~~.041.53 = 75.041.53

6. Metal for etching

   Analysis

Etching (Graphic Art)	762.2
Metal	76.023.3

   Synthesis

   762.2 + ~~76~~.023.3 = 762.2.023.3

7. Medical microscopic photography.

   Analysis

Special applications and techniques of photography	778	
Microscopic photography	77.035	
Medical	61	(to be added with :)

   Synthesis

   778 + ~~77~~.035 + : 61 = 778.035: 61

8. Appreciation of violin music

   Analysis

Violin	787.1
Appreciation	7.073

   Synthesis

   787.1 + ~~7~~.073 = 787.1.073

9. Competitions in stage dance.

   Analysis

Stage dance	792.83
Competition	7.092

Synthesis

792.83 + 7.092 = 792.83.092

10. Endurance capacity in lawn tennis

Analysis

Lawn tennis	796.342
Endurancc capacity	796.012.12

Synthesis

796.342 + 796.012.12 = 796.342.012.12

4.6.8. Language. Linguistics. Literature 8

As already stated in unit 2, the class 4 language and linguistics has been transferred to class 8 literature. The digit 4 has been kept vacant for the time being. The main class 8 includes areas such as : 80 General questions, 81 Linguistics and languages and 82 Literature. In these subject areas we find the use of -1/-9 hyphen series and .01/.09 point nought series of special auxiliary subdivisions. The following worked out examples indicate the use of these two types of special auxiliary subdivisions.

Examples

1. Prague school of Psycholinguistics.

Analysis

Psycholinguistics	81'23
Prague school	81 - 116.3

Synthesis

81'23 + 81 - 116.3 = 81'23 - 116.3

2. Descriptive method of phonetics.

Analysis

Phonetics	81'342
Descriptive method	81 - 133

Synthesis

81'342 + 81 - 133 = 81'342 - 133

3. Characteristic feature of grammar of Sanskrit language

   Analysis

   Sanskrit language 811.211

   Grammar 81‘36

   Characteristic features 81 - 2

   Synthesis

   811.211 + 81’36 + 81 - 2 = 811.211’36 - 2

4. Syntax in modern telugu language

   Analysis

   Telugu language 811.572.24

   Modern 81’06

   Syntax 81’367

   Synthesis

   811.572.24 + 81’06 + 81‘367 = 811.572.24‘06’ ‘367

5. Dictionary of homonyms in Hindi

   Analysis

   Hindi language 811.214.21

   Dictionaries according to vocabulary 81’374.2

   Homonyms 81’373.423

   Synthesis

   811.214.2 + 81’374.2 + 81’373.422

   = 811.214.2’374.2’373.422

6. Aesthetics of Bengali love songs.

   Analysis

   Bengali literature 821.214.32

   Love songs 82 - 146.2

   Aesthetics 111.852 (to be added with :)

   Synthesis

   821.214.32 + 82 - 146.2 + : 111.852

   = 821.214.32 - 146.2 : 111.852

7. Political aspects in Marathi literary essays.

Analysis

Marathi literature	821.214.35	
Essays	82 - 4	
Politics	32	(to be denoted by :)

Synthesis

821.214.35 + 82 - 4 + : 32 = 821.214.35 - 4 + : 32

8. Poetic works of Subrahmanya Bharti, a great tamil poet.

Analysis

Tamil literature	821.573.15	
Poetry	82 - 1	
Subrahmanya Bharati	Bharati	(Alphabetical device)

Synthesis

821.573.15 + 82 - 1 + Bharati = 821.573.15 - 1 Bharati

9. Critism of Gurazada Appa Rao's : Kanyasulkam, a telugu drama.

Analysis

Telugu literature	821.572.24	
Criticism	82.09	
Gurazada Appa Rao	Gurazada	(Alphabetical device)
Kanyasulkam	7 KAN	(Individual works)

Synthesis

821.572.24 + 82.09 + Gurazada + 7KAN

= 821.572.24.09 + Gurazada 7KAN

10. Comparative study of modern malayalam social novels.

Analysis

Malayalam literature	821.573.14
Social novels	82 - 311.4
Modern period	82'06
Comparative study	82.091

Synthesis

821.573.14 + 82'06 + 82 - 311.4 + 82.091

= 821.573.14'06 - 311.4 .091

4.6.9. Geography. Biography. History 9

This main class includes subject areas such as : 902/904 Archaeology, 908 Area studies, 91 Geography, 929 Biographical studies, 93/99 History, 930 Science of history, 931 Ancient history and 94 Medieval and Modern history. There are very few special auxiliary subdivisions provided in this main class. These special auxiliary subdivisions are applied in the following worked out examples.

Examples

1. Recording techniques in under water archaeology.

Analysis

Recording techniques	902.4
Under water archaeology	902.034

Synthesis

902.4 + 902.034 = 902.4.034

2. Weapons of nomadic and pastoral cultures.

Analysis

Weapons	903.22
Nomadic cultures	903'15
Pastoral cultures	903'14

Synthesis

903.22 + 903'15 + 903'14 = 903.22'15'14

3. Forms and shapes of personal ornaments of advanced farming cultures.

Analysis

Personal Ornaments	903.25
Advanced farming cultures	903'16

Forms and shapes 903 - 4

Synthesis

903.25 + ~~903~~'16 + ~~903~~ - 4 = 903.25'16 - 4

4. Dress of Royalty

Analysis

Royalty 929.731

Dress 929.7.038

Synthesis

929.731 + ~~929~~ - 7 .038 = 929.731.038

5. Form of the armorials of civil corporate bodies.

Analysis

Civil corporate bodies 929.647

Form of the armorials 929.64'4

Synthesis

929.647 + ~~929.64~~'4 = 929.647'4

6. Dating techniques in under water building archaeology

Analysis

Dating techniques 902.4

Archaeology according to conditions 902.03

Note : 902.03 ≅ 69.03

As per the above parallel division instruction we have to proceed to 69.03

Under water buildings 69.034.5

Synthesis

902.4 + ~~902~~.0345 = 902.4.0345

Self Check Exercise-5

Classify the following titles.

1. Origins of alphabetical writing systems.
2. Annual reports of non-governmental organisations.
3. Observation of characteristic traits of genius

4. Biological theories of mental disorders.
5. Derived versions of books of Samual.
6. Penances of Jesuits.
7. Public opinion of democracy.
8. State ownership of landed property.
9. Destruction of lakes.
10. Gravity field of Uranus.
11. Tissue structure of nose.
12. Diagnosis of pulmonary complaints.
13. Chinese architecture.
14. Pronouns in modern Assamese.
15. Musical dramas of Oriya.
16. Clothing of pastoral cultures.
17. Insignia of royalty.
18. Silk textile dyeing.
19. Heat treatment of beat sugar.
20. Harvesting equipment for millets.

Note :

(a) Write your answers in the space given below.

(b) Compare your answers with the model answers given at the end of this unit.

....

....

....

....

....

....

....

....

....

....

....

....

....

....

....

....

....

....

....

....

....

4.7. SUMMARY

In the proceeding sections of this unit you have been introduced to the nature and characteristics of special auxiliary subdivisions and their occurrence in common auxiliary subdivisions and the main tables with suitable worked out examples.

Special auxiliary subdivisions unlike common auxiliaries are not listed at one place and their application is some what restricted. The three types of special auxiliary subdivisions viz. 1. -1/-9 hyphen series. 2. .01/.09 point nought series and 3. '1/'9 apostrophe series are listed at various places in tables (schedules) and their application is indicated by instruction, guidance and some times with the suitable worked out examples. These are mainly to be used as suffixes to main UDC class number and cannot be used independently. Of the three types of special auxiliary subdivisions '1/'9 apostrophe series is more specific than -1/-9 and .01/.09. The three types are used either singly or with the combination with other auxiliaries or by citing several auxiliaries with different symbols.

The provision of three types of special auxiliary subdivisions has greatly enhanced synthetic nature and/or number building process in UDC-IME-93. The worked out examples presented in the proceeding sections have greatly demonstrated the value and utility of special auxiliary subdivisions in arriving at co-extensive class numbers.

4.8. ANSWERS TO SELF CHECK EXERCISES

Exercise 1

1. Three ways : 1. Under main class or their subdivisions, 2. Under common auxiliaries, 3. Special auxiliary within a special auxiliary.
2. 1. Common auxiliaries form. Table Id.

   Example : (0.0...) Physical Features. Production...

   2. Common auxiliaries of place. Table Ie.

   Example : (1 - 0/-9) Boundaries and spatial forms of various kinds.
3. 1.Not listed at one place, 2. Occur at various places in the schedules, 3.Applicable only when indicted, 4. Cannot be used independently and 5. Generally listed under a main class.

Exercise 2

1. 616.12 - 072.1
2. 821.214.12 - 146.2
3. 631.334 - 7
4. 314.545.2.026
5. 372.048.2
6. 520.25.02
7. 546.281‘271
8. 637.12‘629.33
9. 811.572.24’374.2’373.423
10. 811.133.1’276

Exercise 3

1. 025.4 UDC.01
2. 061.12.05.064
3. 222/224.063
4. 821.221 - 32
5. 677.372/0373 - 48
6. 616.248 - 07 - 08
7. 546.62'32
8. 811.572.24'34
9. 547.56'032'033
10. 791.43 - 252.03

Exercise 4

1. 575(051.036.4)
2. 551.515.2 (084.35 - 52)
3. 338.45(6 - 772)
4. 795.5(234.075)
5. 553.98(282.253.2Godavari.04)
6. 392.5(=581 - 82)

Exercise 5

1. 003.23.01
2. 061.2.055.6
3. 159.924.2.072.7
4. 159.972.015.7
5. 222.4.043
6. 271.5 - 6
7. 321.7.019.5
8. 332.21.012.332
9. 504.455.056
10. 523.47 - 336
11. 611.21.018

12. 616.24 - 074
13. 72.032.11
14. 811.214.31‘06 - 366.626
15. 821.214.36 - 293.4
16. 903.24’14
17. 929.731.038
18. 677.31.047
19. 664.12.04
20. 633.17 - 35

4.9. ASSIGNMENT

Assign class number to the following titles.

1. Quality of European Standards.
2. Loan services in school libraries.
3. Functions of mathematical logic.
4. Moral values of family ethics.
5. Jewish interpretation of psalms.
6. Preaching orders of montanists.
7. Laws relating to dividends of commercial institutions.
8. Aims and principles of social insurance.
9. Total radiation of x-rays.
10. Gas analysis indicators.
11. Metabolism of enzymes.
12. Mechanically controlled electric machines.
13. Japanese town planning.
14. Morphology of classical Greek.
15. Satirical novels of Punjabi language.
16. Vessels of nomadic cultures.
17. Characteristics of national flag of India.
18. Multifilament polyester fibres.
19. Discoloration of rice flour.
20. Rearing of British mountain sheep.

Unit 5
Synthesis or Number Building Process in UDC

STRUCTURE

5.0. OBJECTIVES

After going through this unit you will be able to :

* understand the meaning of synthesis or number building process in UDC.
* grasp the systematic appratus provided for UDC.
* apply the common an auxiliaries of signs and subdivisions and special auxiliary subdivisions in synthesis or number building process; and
* grasp the scope of parallel division device provided for UDC.

5.1. INTRODUCTION

In the previous three units i.e., 2-4, you have been introduced to the salient features of UDC (IME-93), and the application of common and special auxiliary subdivisions in number building process. The synthetic appratus in UDC constitutes the use of series of symbols and common and special auxiliary subdivisions. The provision of parallel division device also contributed to the synthetic nature of UDC notation. The synthetic apparatus available in UDC is the most powerful apparatus which helps arrive at coextensive class number. This types of synthetic apparatus is rarely found in other general schemes of classification. In the following sections and subsections an attempt has been made to present to you the use of this synthetic apparatus or number building process in UDC (IME)-93.

5.2. MEANING OF SYNTHESIS OR NUMBER BUILDING PROCESS

The word 'synthesis' means the 'construction of compound numbers to denote interrelated subjects that could never be exhaustively foreseen'. It enables to identify various possible relationships between subjects and symbols assigned to represent them. The synthetic principle means that a level of detail could be obtained much greater than what was actually displayed in the tables (schedules). It results in higher precision combined with economy of presentation.

The variety of auxiliary notation consisting signs and subdivisions available in UDC allow for the construction of compound or complex class numbers or synthesis. In addition, the special auxiliary subdivisions and the parallel division device provided in the main tables and auxiliary subdivisions contribute to the synthetic nature of UDC notation. The synthetic apparatus of UDC is presented in subsection 5.2.1.

5.2.1. Synthetic Apparatus in UDC

In UDC we find the most powerful synthetic apparatus available in a series of common and special auxiliary subdivisions which act as systematic mnemonics. The auxiliary subdivisions are well supported by a series of signs which serve as relations linking UDC main or auxiliary number. The following are common auxiliary signs, and subdivisions and special auxiliary subdivisions presented in a tabular form for your easy understanding and grasping.

Table : Synthetic Apparatus in UDC

Symbol	*Name*	*Significance*
A. Common Auxiliary Signs		
+	plus	coordination
/	stroke	consecutive extension
:	colon	simple relation
[ ]	square brackets	subgrouping

: :	double colon	order fixing

B. Common Auxiliary Subdivisions

= ...	Equals	Language-subdivisions
(0 ...)	Bracket nought	form subdivisions
(1/9)	Bracket one to nine	Place Subdivisions
(= ...)	Bracket equals	Ethnic grouping and nationality subdivisions
"..."	Double quotation marks	Time subdivisions
.00...	Point nought-nought	Point of view
-03	Hyphen nought three	Material subdivisions
-05	Hyphen nought five	Persons divisions.

C. Special Auxiliary Subdivisions

-1/-9	Hyphen Series	Limited in scope. To denote recurrent concepts in that part of the main tables for which it is designated.
.01/.09	Point nought series	
'0/'9	Apostrophe series	

As stated already the common auxiliary signs, subdivisions and special auxiliary subdivisions have been dealt in units 3 and 4 with suitable worked out examples. But in the following sections and subsections of this unit you will be demonstrated with worked out examples the part played by these signs and subdivision in achieving synthesis or number building process in classing compound and complex subjects fields.

5.3. COMMON AUXILIARY SIGNS

The common auxiliary signs constitute + the plus, / the stroke, : the colon, [ ] the square brackets and : : double colon. In section I of UDC at page 1 we find these signs.

5.3.1. Coordination, Extension +, /

Table Ia deals with + coordination and / extension. This is further divided into two sections. Section 1 : Coordination and addition. Section 2 : Consecutive extension.

Section 1 : Coordination, Addition, + (Plus)

The coordination sign + plus connects two or more separated i.e., non-consecutive UDC numbers to denote a compound subject for which no single number is available.

Examples

1. Encyclopaedia of Mathematics, Chemistry and Chemical Technology.

Analysis

Maths	51	
Chemistry	54	
Chemical Technology	66	
Encyclopaedia	(031)	from table Id

Synthesis

51 +54 + 66 + (031) = 51 + 54 + 66(031)

2. Report on Economic development in India, Brazil and Australia.

Analysis

Economic development	330.34	
India	(540)	from table le
Brazil	(81)	from table le
Australia	(94)	from table le
Report	(042)	from table Id

Synthesis

330.34 + (540 + 81 + 94) + (042)

= 330.34(540 + 81 + 94) (042)

3. Reference works on documentation, librarianship and journalism in French.

Analysis

Documentation	002
Librarianship	02
Journalism	070

French language	= 133.1	from table Ic
Reference works	(03)	from table Id

Synthesis

022 + 02 + 070 + (03) + = 133.1

= 002 + 02 + 070(03)=133.1

Section 2 : Consecutive Extension / (Stroke)

The extension sign / (stroke) connects the first and the last of a series of consecutive UDC number to denote a broad subject or range of concepts. This sign is very much used in UDC tables (schedules) and we find several examples. The following worked out examples indicate the use of this consecutive extension sign.

Examples

1. Hand book of fundamentals of logic.

Analysis

Fundamentals of logic	161/162	
Hand book	(035)	from table Id

Synthesis

161/162 + (035) = 161/162(035)

2. Micro copies of reports on codification of law of nations.

Analysis

Law of nations	341.1/.8
Codification	341.018
Reports	(047)
Micro copies	(0.035.2)

Synthesis

341.1/08 + 341.018 + (047 + 0.035.2)

= 341.1/.8.018(047.035.2)

3. Survey wall maps on general theory of systematic paleontology in Russian.

Analysis

Systematic Paleontology 562/569

General Theory	56.01	
Wall maps	(084.35)	from table Id
Survey maps	(084.3-37)	from table Id
Russian language	= 161.6	from table Ic

Synthesis

562/569 + 56.01 + (084.35 + 084.3 - 37) = 161.1

= 562/569.01(084.35 - 37) = 161.1

4. Lectures on systematic comparative anatomy in English, Chinese and Japanese.

Analysis

Systematic anatomy	611.1/.8	
Comparative anatomy	611.019	
Lectures	(042.3)	
English	= 111	from table Ic
Chinese	= 581	from table Ic
Japanese	= 521	from table Ic

Synthesis

611.1/.8 + 611.019 + (042.3) + = 111 + = 581 + = 521

= 611.1/.8.019 (042.3) = 111 = 581 = 521

5. Chinese multicolour guide books on glass painting.

Analysis

Glass ware	666.11/.28	
Glass painting	666.1.058.8	
China	(510)	from table Ic
Guide books	(036)	
Multicolour	(0.022.5)	

Synthesis

666.11/.28 + 666.1.05808 + (036 + 0.022.5) + (510)

= 666.11.28.058.8 (036.022.5) (510)

5.3.2. Relation, subgrouping, order fixing :, [ ] , : : (P. 1)

Table Ib of UDC deals with : Relation, [ ] subgrouping and : : order fixing. This table is further divided into these sections: Section 1. Simple relation, Section 2. Subgrouping and Section 3. Order-fixing. The three sections are presented below with suitable worked out examples and clearly demonstrate the synthesis or number building process.

5.3.2.1. Section 1. Simple Relation : (Colon) (P. 1)

The relation sign : (Colon) indicates relationship between two or more subjects connecting their UDC numbers. This is a very dominant and important sign by which we can indicate various types of relations among the subjects in the tables and auxiliary subdivisions as well.

Examples

1. Orations on foreign relations between Russia and France.

Analysis

Foreign relations	327	
Russia	(470)	from table Ie
China	(510)	from table Ie
Orations	(042.5)	

Synthesis

327 + (470 + : 510) + (042.5) = 327 (470 : 510) (042.5)

2. Historical presentation of influence of Sanskrit drama on Telugu drama.

Analysis

Sanskrit drama	821.211-2	
Telugu drama	821.572.24 - 2	(to be added with :)
Historical presentation	(09)	from table Id

Synthesis

821.211 - 2 + : 821.572.24 - 2 + (09)
= 821.211 - 2 : 821.572.24 - 2(09)

3. Religions ethics of Budhism and Hinduism.

   Analysis

Religions ethics	291.5	
Budhism	294.3	(To be added with :)
Hinduism	294.5	

   Synthesis

   291.5 + : 294.3 + 294.5 = 291.5 : 294.3 + 294.5

4. Population policy in relation to demographic situation in India.

   Analysis

Population policy	314.15	
Demographic situation	314.18	
India	(540)	from table Ie

   Synthesis

   314.15 – : 314.18 + (540) = 314.15 : 314.18(540)

5. Situation reports on climatic change and farm production in India.

   Analysis

Climatic change	551.583	
Farm production	631.15	(To be added with :)
Situation reports	(047.1)	
India	(540)	from table Ie

   Synthesis

   551.583 + : 631.15 + (047.1) + (540)
   = 551.583 : 631.15 (047.1) (540)

5.3.2.2. Section 2. Subgrouping [ ] Square brackets (P. 2)

The symbol [ ] square bracket is used as sub-grouping device within a complex combination of UDC numbers. This device is employed when a subject denoted by two or more UDC numbers are linked by plus sign, stroke or colon. In the following worked out examples the use of [ ] is demonstrated to show subgrouping.

Examples

1. International Postal Union

Analysis

Postal services	656.8	
International organisations	061.1	
International	(100)	from table Ie
International postal union	IPU	Alphabetical specification

Synthesis

061.1 + (100) + : [656.8] + IPU

= 061.1(100) : [656.8] IPU

2. Products of cotton and silk textile industry in China and India.

Analysis

Cotton textile	677.21	
Silk textile	677.31	
Products	677.07	
India	(540)	from table Ie
China	(510)	from table Ie

Synthesis

[677.21 + 677.31 + 677.07] + (540 : 510)

= [677.21 + 677.31.07] + (540 : 510)

3. Digital machines in smooth rolling mills for copper in Japan.

Analysis

Digital machines	681.32	
Smooth roll mills	621.771.073	
Copper	669.3	
Japan	(520)	from table Ie

Synthesis

681.32 + : [621.771.073 + : 669.3] + (520)
= 681.32 : [621.771.073 : 669.3] (520)

4. Hindu and Buddhistic religions music.

Analysis

Hinduism	394.5
Budhism	294.3
Religions music	783

Synthesis

783 + : 294.5 9 + + 294.3 = 783 : [294.5 + 294.3]

5. Comparison of Public health services in rural and urban settlement in Bangladesh.

Analysis

Public health	614	
Rural settlements	911.373	
Urban settlements	911.375	
Bangladesh	(549.3)	from table Ie

Synthesis

614 + [911.373 + : 911.375] + (549.3)
= 614[911.373 : 911.375] (549.3)

5.3.2.3. Section 3. Order fixing : : (Double colon) (P. 2)

The symbol : : double colon may be used to fix the order of the component numbers in a compound number especially when the UDC is used in computer based mechanical information system. This is a new connecting sign introduced in IME.

Examples

1. United Nations Educational, Scientific and Cultural Organisation (UNESCO)

Analysis

International Organisation	061.1	
International	(100)	from table Ie

Educational	37	
Scientific	5	
Cultural	008	
United Nations Educational, Scientific and Cultural Organisation	UNESCO	alphabetical specification

Synthesis

061.1 + (100) + : : [37 + 5 + 088] + UNESCO

= 061.1(100) : : [37 + 5 + 008) UNESCO.

2. Hand book Medical jurisprudence

Analysis

Medicine	61	
Jurisprudence	34	
Hand books	(035)	from table Ia

Synthesis

61 + : : + 34 + (035) = 61 : : 34 (035)

3. Molecular systematic zoology.

Analysis

Molecular biology	577
Systematic zoology	592/599

Synthesis

577 + : : 592/599 = 577 : : 592/599.

4. Applied psycho linguistics.

Analysis

Psycholinguistics	81'23
Applied linguistics	81'33

Synthesis

81'33 + : : 81'23 = 81'33 : : 81'23

5. Investigative Journalism

Analysis

Journalism	070
Investigation	343.1

Synthesis

070 + : : 343.1 = 073 : : 343.1

Self Check Exercise - 1

Assign class numbers to the following titles using common auxiliary signs.

1. Practical exercises in classification, cataloging and reference service.
2. Commercial relations between USA and Canada.
3. Encyclopaedia of military affairs in German.
4. Texts for students on mechanics.
5. Tourism in Malaysia and Thailand.
6. Hand book on Hydro-geography.
7. International Institute for cardiology.
8. History and culture of India and Pakistan.
9. Bulletins of Plant Geography.
10. Ecotourism in Sri Lanka.

Note :

(a) Write your answers in the space given below.

(b) Compare your answers with the model answers given at the end of the unit.

....

....

....

....

....

....

....

5.4. COMMON AUXILIARY SUBDIVISIONS

The common auxiliary subdivisions consist of numeric tables in which concepts are enumerated and listed hierarchically. These look like main tables but distinguished by their own symbols either prefixed or enclosing the main number. The time and space common auxiliary subdivisions are common to almost all subject fields. As regards language and form subdivisions they are relevant as soon as a phenomena becomes the subject of the document. These common auxiliary subdivisions are listed at tables Ic to Ik (P. 2-82). These auxiliary subdivisions play vital role in synthesis or number building process in UDC. The following subsections deal with these common auxiliary subdivisions with suitable worked out examples.

5.4.1. Common Auxiliaries of Language, Table Ic (P. 2)

The common auxiliaries of language represent the language or linguistic form of a document whose subject matter or thought content is denoted by main UDC number. These are indicated by the sign = equals in a class number. The following worked out examples demonstrate the part played by language subdivisions in synthesis or number building process in UDC.

Example

1. Agricultural chemical industries; a reference book in Swedish language.

   Analysis

Manufacturing industries	338.45	
Agricultural chemicals	661.15	(to be added with :)
Reference book	(03)	
Swedish language	= 113.6	

   Synthesis

   338.4 + : 661.15 + (03) + = 113.6

   = 338.4 : 661.15 (03) = 113.6

2. C.P. Brown's English - Telugu dictionary.

Analysis

Dictionaries	(038)
English language	= 111
Telugu language	= 572.24

Synthesis

(038) + = 111 + = 572.24 = (038) = 111 = 572.24

3. Etymological dictionary of classical tamil, telugu and sanskrit.

Analysis

Languages	811
Tamil	= 573.15
Telugu	= 572.24
Sanskrit	= 211
Etymology	81'373.614
Dictionary	(038)

Synthesis

811 + = 211 + = 573.15 + = 572.15 + 81'373.614 + (038)

= 811 = 211 = 573.15 = 572.15'373.614(038)

4. Bengali novels translated in to telugu.

Analysis

Bengali literature	821.214.32
Novels	82 - 31
Translations	= 03
Telugu language	= 572.24

Synthesis

821.214.32 + 82 - 31 + = 03 + = 572.24

= 821.214.32 - 31 = 03 = 572.24

5. Modern Hindi couplets dictionary.

Analysis

Hindi language	811.214.21

Modern	'06	
Couplets	801.67	(to be added with :)
Dictionary	(038)	

Synthesis

811.214.21 + '06 + : 801.67 + (038)

= 811.214.21'06 : 801.67(038)

6. Multivolume encyclopaedia of North Indian Hindi dialects.

Analysis

Hindi language	811.214.21	
Regional dialects	81'282.3	
Multi volume Encyclopaedia	(031.038)	
North India	(545)	from table Ie

Synthesis

811.214.21 + 81'<u>282.3</u> + (545) + (031.038)

= 811.214.21'<u>282.3</u> (545)(031.038)

5.4.2. Common Auxiliaries of Form. Table Id

The common auxiliaries of form or presentation of documents is represented by the symbol (0...) brackets nought. These are not used to denote the subject matter of the documents. You have been already introduced to this table under unit 2, section 2.6.2 and unit 3, section 3.3.2. The following worked out examples demonstrate the role played by common auxiliaries of form in synthesis or number building process in UDC along with other common auxiliary subdivisions.

Examples

1. Oxford university press paper back editions price list.

Analysis

Publishing	655.41
Oxford University Press	OUP(alphabetical specification)
Price list	(085.6)

Paper back editions (0.027.5)

Synthesis

655.41 + 001 + (085.6 + Ø.027.5)
= 655.41OUP (085.6.0275.5)

2. English-French miniature Medical Dictionary.

Analysis

Medicine	61
Dictionary	(038)
Miniature edition	(0.021.6)
English	= 111
French	= 133.1

Synthesis

61 + (038 + Ø.021.6) + = 111 + = 133.1
= 61(038.021.6) = 111 = 133.1

3. Monthly domestic science journal for women.

Analysis

Domestic science	64	
Monthly journal	(051)	
Documents for women	(0.055.2)	
Monthly	"540.1"	from table Ig

Synthesis

64 + (051 + Ø.055.2) + "540.1" = 64(051.055.2) "540.1"

4. Survey of India, survey maps.

Analysis

Cartography	528.9	(to be added with :)
Survey of India	SI	(alphabetical specification)
Govt. organisations (National)	061.1	
India	(540)	
Survey maps	(084.3 - 37)	

Synthesis

061.1(540) + SI + : 528.9 + (084.3 - 37)
= 061.1(540)SI : 528.9SI(084.3 - 37)

5. Greeting cards associated with India's independence day 15th August.

Analysis

Greeting cards	(089.7)
August 15, (Independence day) in India	"383:327.08.15" (540)

Synthesis

(089.7) + "383 : 327.08.15" (540)
= (089.7) "383 : 327.08.15" (540)

Note : The above compound number can be attached to relevant UDC class number.

6. Political biographies presented in poetry form.

Analysis

Political science	32	
Biography	929	(to be added with :)

Note : Under table Id at page 15 you will find the following note "Kinds of form not listed in table Id may be denoted by (0:...).

Synthesis

32 + : 929 + (0 : 82 - 1) = 32 : 929(0 : 82 - 1)

5.4.3. Common Auxiliaries of place, Table Ie

The common Auxiliaries of place indicate the geographical range, locality or other spatial aspects of a subject denoted by main UDC number. These are indicated by the symbol (1/9) brackets one to nine. You have been already introduced to common auxiliaries of place in unit 2, section 2.6.3 and unit 3, section 3.3.3. In the following worked out examples the role played by common auxiliaries of place in synthesis or number building process is demonstrated.

Examples

1. Indo-US nuclear deal in 2006.

Analysis

Nuclear energy	621 039
U.S.A.	(73)
India	(540)
2006	"2006"

Synthesis

621.039 (540 : 73) "2006"

2. Rural employment guarantee scheme in Andhra Pradesh.

Analysis

Employment service	331.532
Andhra Pradesh	(548.23)
Rural area	(1 - 22)

Synthesis

331.532 + (548.23 + 1 - 22) = 331.532 (548.23 - 22)

3. Cultural relations between ancient Egypt and India during first century A.D.

Analysis

Culture	008	
Ancient Egypt	(32)	
Ancient India	(34)	
First Century A.D.	"00"	from table Ig

Synthesis

088 + (32 + : 34) "00" = 088 (32 : 34) "00"

4. Blue whale hunting in the North Atlantic Ocean region of Europe during summer.

Analysis

Hunting marine mammals	639.24

Note : 639.245/.247 ≅ 599.5/.7

Blue whale	599.511	
Blue whale hunting	639.245 + 599.511 i.e., 639.245.11	
North Atlantic Ocean	(261.1)	
Europe	(4)	
Summer	"322"	from table Ig

Synthesis

639.245.11 + (4 + - 261.1) + "322"

= 639.245.11 (4 - 261.1) "322"

5. Mineral resources and reserves in SAARC countries.

Analysis

Mineral resources and reserves	553.04	
Countries with market economy	(1 - 672)	
South Asia	(54)	
South Asian Association for Regional cooperation	SAARC	(alphabetical specification)

Synthesis

553.04(54 + 1 - 672 + SAARC) = 553.04(54 - 672 SAARC)

6. Exploration of Ice caps of North Polar circle.

Analysis

Exploration	910.3
Ice caps	551.324.24 (to be added with :)
Polar circle	(160.25)
North	(1 - 17)

Synthesis

910.3 + : 551.324 + (160.25 + 1 - 17)

= 910.3 : 551.324 (160.25 - 17)

Self Check Exercise - 2

Assign class numbe- to the following titles.

1. A Guide to Dewey Decimal Classification in English, French and German.
2. League of Nations documents translated from Dutch into Portuguese.
3. Hand book of classificatory language in Hindi.
4. Ess Ess Publications : Library Science Books, hardback editions.
5. Multi volume encyclopaedias on religion and ethics.
6. Historical biographies presented in novel form.
7. Indian Russian defence cooperation during 1960's
8. Mountaineering in the Western Himalayas during summer 1953.
9. Harvesting of wheat in rural areas of north India during December 2005.
10. Small agrarian societies in the states of India.

Note :

(a) Write your answer in the space given below.

(b) Compare your answers with the model answers given at the end of this unit.

....

....

....

....

....

....

....

....

....

....

....

5.4.4. Common Auxiliaries of Ethnic grouping and Nationality. Table If (P. 65)

The common auxiliaries of ethnic grouping and nationality represent the nationality or ethnic aspects of a subject represented by main UDC class number. The symbol (= ...) bracket equal denote these common auxiliaries in the class number. You have been already introduced to this table in unit 2, section 2.6.4 and unit 3, section 3.3.4. The following worked out examples will demonstrate the role of these auxiliaries in synthesis or number building process in UDC.

Examples

1. Wages for native Nepalese in India.

Analysis

Wages	331.2	
Natives	(=1 - 82)	
Nepal	(541.35)	from table Ie
India	(540)	from table Ie

Synthesis

331.2 + (=1.541.35 + *1* - <u>82</u>) (540)

= 331.2 (=1.541.35 - <u>82</u>) (540)

2. Illustrated documents on head gear of ancient Romans and Greeks.

Analysis

Head gear	646.5
Ancient Romans	(= 1.37)
Ancient Greeks	(= 1.38)
Illustrated documents	(084.1)

Synthesis

646.5 + (=1.37 + = 1.38) + (084.1)

= 646.5 (=1.37 + = 1.38) (084.1)

3. Persecution of Jews in Germany during second world war.

Analysis

Racialism	323.14
Jews	(= 411.16)
Germany	(430)
Second world war (1939/1945)	940.53

Synthesis

323.14 + (=411.16) + (430) + : 940.53

= 323.14(=411.16) (430) : 940.53

or

323.14 (=411.16) (430) "1939/1945"

4. History of social customs of telugu people.

Analysis

Social customs	391	
Telugu people	(=572.24)	from table Ic
History	(091)	from table Id

Synthesis

391 + (=572.24) + (091) = 391 (=572.24) (091)

5. Historical accounts of Voyages of ancient Persians and Mesopotamians.

Analysis

Voyages	910.4	
Ancient Persians	(=1.355)	
Ancient Mesopotamians	(=1/358)	
Historical account	(091)	from table Id

Synthesis

910.4 + (= 1.355 + = 1.358) + (091)

= 910.4 (= 1.355 + = 1.358) (091)

6. Social development of high mountain dwellers of Himachal Pradesh.

Analysis

Social development 316.42

High Mountain dwellers (=1.23.03)

Himachal Pradesh (545.4) from table Ie

Synthesis

316.42 + (=1.23.03) + (545.4) = 316.42 (=1.23.03) (545.4)

5.4.5. Common Auxiliaries of Time. Table Ig (P. 66)

The common Auxiliaries of time denote point of time or range of time of a subject represented by main UDC class number. The schedule is drawn on the basis of Christian calender. The non-Christian religious time reckoning is provided at "68" and "69". You have been already introduced to common auxiliaries of time in unit 2, section 2.6.5 and Unit 3, section 3.3.5. UDC provides for very minute time divisions to represent various aspects of time. The following worked out example demonstrate the role of these auxiliary division in synthesis or number building process.

Examples

1. Hindu time reckoning according to Mahabharata.

Analysis

Mahabharata 294.118

Non-christian religion time reckoning "69"

Note : "69" ≅ 59

Hinduism 294.5

Hindu time reckoning "69 + 294.5 = "694.5"

Synthesis

294.118 + : "694.5" = 294.118 "694.5"

2. Mango harvesting in Summer 2006.

Analysis

Mango	634.441
Harvesting	634.8.07

Note : The .0 special auxiliaries listed under 634.8.0... are also applicable throughout 634" (Page 619)

2006	"2006"
Summer	"322"

Synthesis

634.441 + 634.07 + "2006.322" = 634.441.07 "2006.322"

3. Cricket championship matches between India and Pakistan during Jan.-Feb. 2006.

Analysis

Cricket	796.358	
Championships	796.093.426	
India	(540)	from table Ie
Pakistan	(549.1)	from table Ie
2006	= "2006"	
Jan/Feb.	"01/02"	

Synthesis

796.358 + 796.093.426 − (540 + : 549.1) + 2006.01/.02 =
796.358.093.426(540 : 549.1) "2006.01/02"

4. Launching of rural health programme during 15th August (independence day) in India.

Analysis

Rural health	614.79	
National holiday	"383"	from table Ig.
Month of the year	"327"	from table Ig.
15th August	"08.15"	from table Ig.
India	(540)	from table Ie

Synthesis

614.79 + "383" + : "327 + 08.15" (540)

= 614.79 "383 : 327.08.15"(540)

5. Reptiles remains of Jurassic period.

   Analysis

Reptiles (Paleozoology)	568.1	
Jurassic period	"6152"	from table Ig

   Synthesis

   568.1 + "6152" = 568.1 "6152"

6. Agrarian conditions during the middle ages in China.

   Analysis

Agrarian conditions	338.43.1	
China	(510)	from table Ie
Middle ages	"653"	from table Ig

   Synthesis

   338.431 + (510) + "653" = 338.431 (510) "653"

5.4.6. Subject specification by Notations from Non-UDC Sources. Table Ih (P. 73)

This table specifies means of adding non-UDC notation by using * asterisk which is not an authorised UDC number. Likewise alphabetical specification by proper names (or their abbreviations) and acronyms, the letter notation A/Z may be added direct to the UDC base number. The symbols * and A/Z help to achieve synthesis or number building process in UDC. You have been already introduced to subject specification by non-UDC sources in unit 2, section 2.7.4 and unit 3, section 3.4.4. The following are few more worked out examples which demonstrate the role of * and A/Z in number building process in UDC.

Examples

1. Kolkata tram way. Route No. 20.

Analysis

Tram ways	625.46	
Kolkata	(540 - 25 KOL)	from table Ie
Route No. 20	*20	

Synthesis

625.46 + (540 + 25KOL) +*20

= 625.46 (540 + 25KOL)*20

2. 212° F (Boiling Point of Water)

Analysis

Temperature	66 - 97
212° F	*F212

Synthesis

66 - 97 + * F 212 = 66 - 97 * F 212.

3. 500 KMs cross country motor cycle racing.

Analysis

Motor cycling	796.72
Cross country	796.093.55
500 KMs	*KM500

Synthesis

796.72 + ~~796~~.093.55 + *KM500 = 796.72.093.55 *KM500

4. Annual report of International Atomic Energy Agency (IAEA)

Analysis

Atomic Energy	621.039	
International organisations	061.1	
International	(100)	from table Ie
Int. Atomic Energy Agency	IAEA	(Alphabetical specification)

Annual report (047) from table Id

Synthesis

061.1 + (100) + : 621.039 + IAEA + (047)
= 061.1 (100) : 621.039 IAEA (047)

5. Works of Sumitranandan Pant.

Analysis

Hindi literature 821.214.21

Sumitranandan Pant Pant(alphabetical specification)

Synthesis

821.214.21 + Pant = 821.214.21 Pant

6. Biography of S. Radha Krishnan.

Analysis

Biography 929

S. Radha Krishnan Radha Krishnan or Radha (alphabetical specification)

Synthesis

929 + Radha = 929 Radha

Self Check Exercise - 3

Assign class numbers to the following titles.

1. Living conditions of native Bangladeshis in West Bengal.
2. Sketches of Footwear of ancient Britains and Spaniards.
3. Tropical Climatic indications by Indian Standard Time (IST)
4. Midnight airmail service.
5. Elevated railway service in Tokyo. Route No. 100.
6. 20 KM walking competition.
7. Annual report of Indira Gandhi Atomic Research Centre, Kalpakkam for the year 2005.
8. National Mineral Development corporation, India.

Note :

(a) Write your answers in the space given below.

(b) Compare your answers with the model answers given at the end of this unit.

....

....

....

....

....

....

5.4.7. Common Auxiliaries of Point of View. Table Ii (P. 73)

These auxiliaries represent most general points of view which a subject may be considered. These are applicable throughout the scheme especially in the main classes, Sciences 5, Technology 6 and the Arts 7. These are not used independently or cited first in the compound class number of UDC. These can be used as suffixes to a main UDC class number. These auxiliaries play a vital role in synthesis or number building process. You have been already introduced to common auxiliaries of point of view in unit 2, section 2.7.1 and unit 3, section 3.4.1. The following are some more worked out examples.

Examples

1. Telugu poetry discussed from optimism view point.

Analysis

Telugu poetry	821.572.24 - 1
Note : .000.0/.9 ≅ 0/9	(Page 74)
Optimism	141.21 i.e., .000.141.21

Synthesis

821.572.24 - 1 + .000.141.21 = 821.572.24 - 1.000.141.21

2. Hyderabad city master plan.

Analysis

Capital cities (Town planning)	711.432	
Hyderabad city	(548.23 - 25 HYD)	from table Ie
Master plan	.001.14	from table Ii

Synthesis

711.432 + .001.14 + (548.23 - 25 HYD)
= 711.432.001.14 (548.23 - 25 HYD)

3. Advantages of automation in Public Libraries.

Analysis

Public libraries	027.4	
Automation	681.5	(to be added with :)

Advantage point of view.004.122

Synthesis

027.4 + .004.122 + : 681.5 = 0270.4.004.122 : 681.5

4. Chain saws (mine excavation) as tools.

Analysis

Chain saws	622.23.054.7
Tools (point of view)	.002.54

Synthesis

622.23.054.7 + .002.54 = 622.23.054.7.002.54

5. Flower exports - profit point of view.

Analysis

Flowers	631.575	
Profit point of view	.003.8	
Exports	339.564	(to be added with :)

Synthesis

631.575 + .003.8 + : 339.564 = 631.575.003.8 : 339.564

6. Savings banks relations with customers.

Analysis

Saving banks	336.72
Relations with customers (point of view)	.009.7

Synthesis

336.72 + .009.7 = 336.72.009.7

5.4.8. Common Auxiliaries of General Characteristics. Table Ik (P. 76)

Under Table Ik two common auxiliary tales have been provided. These are : -03 common Auxiliaries of Materials and -05 Common Auxiliaries of persons and personal characteristics. This table has been newly introduced in UDC-IME-1985 and continue in UDC-IME-1993 Edition. These two tables have greatly contributed to the enhancement of synthesis or number building process in UDC. These two common auxiliary tables is presented in the following subsections.

5.4.8.1. Common Auxiliaries of Materials -03, (P. 76)

These common auxiliaries denote materials or constituents of which objects or products are made. The symbol - 03 hyphen nought three indicates the common auxiliaries of materials in the class number. These are applicable throughout the main tables of UDC if the material aspect is secondary to the subject. These are not to be used independently or cited first in the compound class number. You have been already introduced to common auxiliarics of materials in unit 2, section 2.7.2 and unit 3, section 3.4.2. The following are some more worked out examples which demonstrate the synthesis or number building nature in UDC with the help of -03 common auxiliaries of materials.

Examples

1. Cutlery in bamboo.

   Analysis

   Cutlery 642.73

   Bamboo -035.26

   Synthesis

   642.73 + - 035.26 = 642.73 - 035.26

2. Leather book binding.

   Analysis

   Book binding 686.1

Leather - 035.51 from table Ik

Synthesis

686.1 + - 035.51 = 686.1 - 035.51

3. Gold and copper metals for head jewellery manufacturing.

Analysis

Head jewellary	671.123	
Gold	- 032.42	from table Ik
Copper	- 034.3	from table Ik

Note : Composite materials may be denoted by apostrophe combination in which the apostrophe replaces -03 in the second and subsequent component numbers" (P. 76). Hence :

Gold and Copper - 032.42 + -~~03~~4.3 = - 032.42'43

Synthesis

671.123 + - 032.42'43 = 671.123 - 032.42'43

4. Bricks and Cement for Industrial building.

Analysis

Industrial buildings	725.4	
Cement	- 033.24	from table Ik
Bricks	- 033.71	from table Ik
Composite material	- 033.24 + - ~~03~~3.71 = 033.24'371	

Synthesis

725.4 + - 033.24'371 = 725.4 - 033.24'371

5. Bamboo and soft wood for news print industry.

Analysis

News print industry	676.222	
Bamboo	- 035.26	from table Ik
Soft wood	-035.32	from table Ik
Composite material	-035.26 + -~~03~~5.32 = 035.26'532	

Synthesis

676.22 + -035.26'532 = 676.222 - 035.26'532

6. Synthetic and metal fibres for clothing industry.

Analysis

Clothing industry	687	
Synthetic fibres	-0.37.47	from table Ik
Metal fibres	- 037.53	from table Ik
Composite material	-037.47 + -0<u>37.53</u> = -037.47'<u>753</u>	

Synthesis

687 + - 037.47'753 = 687 - 037.47'753

5.4.8.2. Common Auxiliaries of persons and Personal characteristics - 05 (P. 78)

The common auxiliaries of persons and personal characteristics denote persons concerned or their characteristics but not things or disciplines according to personal application. They symbol -05 hyphen nought five indicate the persons in the UDC class number. These are applicable throughout the main tables if the personal aspect is secondary to the subject. These are not to be used independently or cited first in a compound class number. You have been already introduced to this table in unit 2, section 2.7.3 and unit 3, section 3.4.3. The following few more worked out examples demonstrate the use of common auxiliaries of persons in synthesis or number building process in UDC.

Examples

1. Biography Physicists.

Analysis

Physics	53	
Persons	-05	from table Ik
Biography	(092)	from table Id

Synthesis

53 + - 05 + (092) = 53 - 05 (092)

2. Social conditions of Indic races and Peoples.

Analysis

Social conditions	332.158	
Persons according to ethnic characteristics	-054	from table Ik
Indic races and peoples	(=21)	from table If

Synthesis

332.158 + - 054 + (=21) = 332.158 - 054 (=21)

3. Gifted Indian chess players.

Analysis

Chess	794.1	
Gifted persons	-056.45	from table Ik
Indians	(=1.540)	from table If

Synthesis

794.1 + - 056.45 + (= 1.540) = 794.1 - 056.45 (= 1.540)

4. Directory of middle aged male teachers.

Analysis

Education	37	
Middle aged	- 053.88	from table Ik
Male	- 055.1	from table Ik
Directory	(058)	from table Id

Synthesis

37 + - 053.88 + -055.1 + (058) = 37 - 053.88 - 055.1 (058)

5. Rehabilitation assistance to child orphans in Andhra Pradesh.

Analysis

Rehabilitation assistance	364.048.6	
Children	-053.2	
Orphans	- 058.862	
Andhra Pradesh	(548.4)	from table Ie

Synthesis

364.048.6 + - 053.2 + - 058.862

= 364.048.6 - 053.2 - 058.862

6. Statistics of victims of road traffic accidents in Mumbai city.

Analysis

Official statistics	311.312	
Road traffic accidents	656.1.08	
Victims of disasters	- 058.66	from table Ik
Mumbai city	(547.1 - 25 MUM)	

Synthesis

311.312 + : 656.1.08 + - 058.66 (547.1 - 25 MUM)

= 311.312 : 656.1.08 - 058.66 (547.1 - 25 MUM)

Self Check Exercise - 4

Assign class numbers to the following titles.

1. Hindi poetry from sufism point of view.
2. Textile exports : Economic point of view.
3. Table ware in silver and copper.
4. Metal fibres for fishing nets.
5. Collective biography of eminent chemical engineers of India.
6. Gifted Indian young cricket players.

Note :

(a) Write your answers in the space given below.

(b) Compare your answers with the model answers given at the end of this unit.

....

....

....

....

....

....

5.5. SPECIAL AUXILIARY SUBDIVISIONS. (SECTION II. P. 83)

As the term indicates the special auxiliary subdivisions viz., hyphen series -1/-9, Point nought series .01/.09 and apostrophe series '0/'9 are limited in their scope and application. Each of these series is used to denote recurrent concepts in that part of the main schedule. Unlike common auxiliary subdivision, in special auxiiiary subdivision the same notation is used with different meanings in different places in the schedules. The three types of special auxiliary subdivisions have greatly contributed the synthetic nature in UDC. You have been already introduced to the application of special auxiliaries in unit 2, section 2.8. The entire unit 4 deals with three types of special auxiliary subdivisions. In the following subsections some more worked out examples is presented using the three types of special auxiliary subdivisions. These worked out examples demonstrate the role of these subdivisions in achieving synthesis or number building in UDC.

5.5.1. Hyphen Series -1/-9 (P. 83)

The hyphen series -1/-9 are mainly analytical in nature and indicate elements, components, properties and other details of the subject denoted by main UDC class number to which they apply. These are listed at different places in the schedules but specially at 62/69 and 82. You have been already introduced to the application of hyphen series of special auxiliaries in unit 2, section 2.8.1 and in unit 4, section 4.3.1. The following are some more worked out examples which demonstrate the role of hyphen series in synthesis or number building process in UDC.

Examples

1. Use of computers in statistical analysis.

Analysis

Statistical analysis	519.23
Use of computers in mathematics	51 - 37

Synthesis

519.23 + ~~81~~ - 37 = 519.23 - 37

2. Surgical treatment of liver cancer.

Analysis

Liver	616.36
Cancer	616 - 006.6
Surgical treatment	616 - 089

Synthesis

616.36 + ~~616~~ - 006.6 + ~~616~~ - 089 = 616.36 - 006.6 - 089

3. Graft of skin taken from hips on the legs.

Analysis

Skin	616.5
Grafting	616 - 089.843

Note : See instruction under 616 - 089.843 at page 427.

Hips	611.96 + - 032
Legs	611.98

Synthesis

616.5 + ~~616~~ - 089.843 + :611.96 + - 032 + : 611.98
= 616.5 - 089.843 : 611.96 - 032 : 611.98

4. Threaded fasteners for drilling machines.

Analysis

Drilling machines	621.925
Fastening	62 - 238

Note : 62 - 238 ≅ 621.88

As per the above parallel division instruction we have to proceed to 621.88

Threaded fasteners	621.882
i.e.,	62 - 238 + ~~621.88~~ 2 = 62 - 238.2

Synthesis

621.925 + ~~62~~ - 238.2 = 621.925 - 238.2

5. Virus diseases of potatoes.

   Analysis

Potatoes	633.49

   Note : At page 616 under 633 - 1/-2 we find the following instruction. "The 62 - 1 ... and 62.2 auxiliaries are not applicable at 633 and its subdivisions 633 - 1/-2 ≅ 631/ 632.

Virus diseases	632.38 i.e., 633 - 38

6. Super fine, high strength portland cement.

   Analysis

Portland cement	666.942
Super fine	666.9 - 121
High strength	666.9 - 16

   Synthesis

   666.942 + ~~666.9~~ - 121 + ~~666.9~~ - 16 = 666.942 - 121 - 16

5.5.2. Point nought Series .01/.09 (P. 83)

The point nought series is more diversely used and developed in much more detail than -1/-9. This series represent recurrent concepts such as : aspect studies, activities, processes, operations, plant and equipments. These are listed at different places in the schedules especially under the classes such as 35, 71/79, 8 and 9. The point nought series have greatly contributed to the synthesis or number building quality in UDC. The following worked out examples have demonstrated this quality of synthesis. You have been already introduced to the point nought series in unit 2, section 2.8.2 and unit 4, section 4.3.2.

Examples

1. Transliteration of Devanagari script into South Indian script.

   Analysis

Devanagari script	003.336.3
Transliteration	003.34

South Indian scripts (to be added with :)	003.336.6

Synthesis

033.336.3 + ~~003~~.034 + : 033.366.6
= 033.336.3.034 : 033.366.6

2. Subject and verbal concordances of New Testament.

Analysis

New Testament	225
Verbal concordances	22.03
Subject concordances	22.032

Synthesis

225 + ~~22~~.03 + ~~22~~.032 = 225.03.032

3. Moral and Material support for Agricultural Cooperatives.

Analysis

Cooperative companies	334.73
Agricultural cooperatives	631.115.8 (to be added with :)
Material support	334.027
Moral support	334.028

Synthesis

334.73 + : 631.115.8 + ~~334~~.027 + ~~334~~.028
= 334.73 : 631.115.8.027.028

4. Biological and Chemical effects of rarefied gases.

Analysis

Rarefied gases	533.5
Chemical effects	53.004
Biological effects	53.047

Synthesis

533.5 + ~~53~~.044 + ~~53~~.047 = 533.5.044.047

5. Predators as enemies to Sardines.

   Analysis

   Sardines 639.222.5

   Enemies of fish 639.2.09

   Note : 639.2.09 ≅ 639.1.09

   Predators 639.1.092 i.e., 639.2.092

   Synthesis

   639.222.5 + ~~639~~.2.092 = 639.22.5.092

6. Gas purification by adsorption and desorption.

   Analysis

   Gas purification methods 66.074.5

   Note : Denote methods not given 66.074.5/.9 by adding other auxiliaries from 66 (P. 692)

   Adsorption 66.081.3

   Desorption 66.081.5

   Synthesis

   66.074.5 + ~~66~~.081.3 + ~~66~~.081.5 = 66.074.5.081.3.081.5

5.5.3. Apostrophe Series '0/'9 (P. 83)

The apostrophe series is more specific than hyphen and point nought series. These are synthetic or integrative in nature representing compound subjects by compound notation. This series is profusely used in the classes 329, 54, 669 and 81. You have been already introduced to apostrophe series in unit 2, section 2.8.3 and unit 4, section 4.3.3. The following worked out examples demonstrative the role of apostrophe series in synthesis or number building process in UDC.

Examples

1. Asymmetric and symmetric aromatic compounds.

   Analysis

   Aromatic compounds 547.52

   Asymmetric 547.52'032

Symmetric 547.52'033

Synthesis

547.52 + ~~547.52~~'032 + ~~547.52~~'.033 = 547.52'032'033.

2. Organic compounds of selenium, boron and silicon.

Analysis

Organic compounds	547.1
Selenium	547.1'123
Boron	547.1'127
Silicon	547.1'128

Synthesis

547.1 + ~~547.1~~'123 + ~~547.1~~'127 + ~~547.1~~'128

= 547.1'123'127'128

3. Phonology of modern arabic.

Analysis

Arabic language	811.411.21
Modern	81'06
Phonology	81'34

Synthesis

811.411.21 + ~~81~~ + '06 + ~~81~~ '34 = 811.411.21'06 '34

4. Homonyms and synonyms of classical Sanskrit.

Analysis

Sanskrit language	811.211
Classical period	81'02
Homonyms	81'373.423
Synonyms	81'373.421

Synthesis

811.211 + ~~81~~'02 + ~~81~~'373.421 + ~~81~~'373.423

= 811.211'02 '373.421 '373.423

5. Clothing of nomadic and Pastoral cultures.

   Analysis

Clothing	903.24
Nomadic culture	903'15
Pastoral culture	903'14

   Synthesis

   903.24 + ~~903~~'14 + ~~903~~'15 = 903.24'14'15

6. Liberal republican attitude political parties.

   Analysis

Liberal attitude	329.12
Republic attitude	329.23

   Synthesis

   329.12 + ~~329~~'23 = 329.12'23

   Note : See note under 329.1/-6 at page 149)

5.6. Parallel Divisions

The most important synthetic device introduced in the UDC-IME is parallel divisions indicated by the symbol ≅ at various points in the schedules. This device indicates that the number proceeding ≅ may be subdivided in a manner analogous to the number following it. This device ensures that the same notation is being used to denote a given concept in more than one place. We will find this device not only in the main tables (Schedules) but also in common and special auxiliary tables. You have been already introduced to this concept in unit 2, section 2.9.2. The following are some more examples of use of parallel divisions which demonstrate the synthetic nature in UDC.

Examples

1. Ethics of hinduism.

   Analysis

Characters and elements of hinduism	294.51

   Note : 294.51 ≅ 291

Religious Ethics 291.5

Synthesis

294.51 + 291.5 = 294.515

2. Monetary support by social security insurance.

Analysis

Social security insurance 369.8

Note : 369.8 ≅ 364.42

Monetary support 364.422

Synthesis

369.8 + ~~364.42~~2 = 369.82

3. Legal documents in morocco leather.

Analysis

Law 34

Documents according to material (Substance) (0.023)

(0.023) ≅ - 03 (Table Ik)

Morocco leather - 035.513 from table Ik

i.e., (0.023 + - 035.513 = (0.023.551.3)

Synthesis

34 + (0.023.551.3) = 34(0.023.551.3)

4. Evolutionary theory from the Buddhistic point of view.

Analysis

Evolution 575.8

General approach outlook .000.0/.9

.000.0/.9 ≅ 0/9

Budhism 294.3

Synthesis

575.8 + .000. + 294.3 = 575.8.000.294.3

5. Restrictions on members of national organisations in India.

Analysis

National organisations 061.1

Matters concerning members	06.028 06.028 ≅ 35.078
Restrictions	35.078.1
i.e.,	06.028 + 35.078.1 = 06.028.1

Synthesis

061.1 + .06.028.1 = 061.1.028.1

6. Hyperactivity of lungs.

Analysis

Lungs	616.24
Specific functions of individual organs	616 - 008.1 616 - 008.1 ≅ 616 - 008.6
Hyper activity	616 - 008.61

i.e., 616 - 008.1 + ~~616~~ - ~~00~~8.61 = 616 - 008.11

Synthesis

616.24 + ~~616~~ - 008.11 = 616.24 - 008.11

Self Check Exercise - 5

Assign class numbers to the following titles.

1. Tooth extraction.
2. Electronically controlled turbo pumps.
3. Regulators aspects of land use of forestry.
4. Care and rearing methods of goats.
5. Potassium Cyanide and Borate.
6. Modern telugu dialects.
7. Religions duties of Lamaism.
8. Class teachers for vocational training.

Note :

(a) Write your answers in the space given below.

(b) Compare your answers with the model answers given at the end of this unit.

....

....

....

....

....

....

....

....

....

5.7. SUMMARY

Synthesis means the construction of compound numbers to denote inter related subjects that could never be exhaustively foreseen. The variety of auxiliary notation consisting signs and subdivisions available in UDC allow for the construction of compound and complex numbers. The synthetic apparatus available in UDC is in the form of common auxiliary signs and subdivisions and special auxiliary subdivisions which act as systematic mnemonics. In addition the provision of parallel divisions at several places in the schedules has greatly contributed to the synthetic or number building process in UDC. The systematic process in UDC has been amply demonstrated by the worked out examples presented in the proceeding sections of this unit.

5.8. ANSWERS TO SELF-CHECK EXERCISES

Exercise - 1

1. 025.4 + 025.3 + 027.081 (076.5)
2. 339.1(73:71)
3. 355/359 (031) = 112
4. 531/534(075)
5. 910.4(595 + 593)
6. 911.2 : 556 (035)
7. 061.1 (100) : [612.17] IIC

8. [93/99 + 008] (540 + 549.1)
9. 911.2 : : 581.9 (047)
10. 574 : : 910.4 (548.7)

Exercise - 2

1. 025.45DDC (038) = 111 = 122.2 = 133.1
2. 341.121 = 03.112.5 = 134.3
3. 81'276.6 : 025.4 = 21 (035)
4. 655.41 SSP : 02 (0.026.2)
5. 2 + 17 (031.038)
6. 93/99 : 929 (0 : 82 - 31)
7. 355/359 (540 : 470) "196"
8. 796.525 (235.243 - 15) "1953.322"
9. 631.558 : 633.11 (545 - 22) "2005.12.00"
10. 316.324.5.023.4(540 - 43)

Exercise - 3

1. 364.252(=1.549.3 - 82) (541.23)
2. 646.6 (= 1.366 + = 1.365) (084.11)
3. 551.581.24 "317" IST
4. 656.7:659.138.6"3455"
5. 656.34(520 - 25 Tokyo) * 100
6. 796.421.093 - KM 20
7. 061.1(540 - 25 KAL) : 621.039IARC(047)"2005"
8. 061.1(540) : 553NMDC

Exercise-4

1. 821.214.21 - 1.000.141.336
2. 677 : 339.564.003.1
3. 642.7 - 032.42 - 034.3
4. 639.2081.11 - 037.53
5. 66 - 05(540) (092) (08)

6. 796.358 - 056.45 - 053.81(540)

Exercise-5

1. 616.314 - 089.87
2. 621.675 - 523.8
3. 332.334.4 : 630.024
4. 636.39.083.31
5. 546.32‘267’273
6. 811.572.25‘06’282
7. 294.321.5
8. 377.121.31

5.9. ASSIGNMENT

Assign class numbers to the following titles.

1. Introduction to physics, chemistry and chemical technology.
2. Manual on bibliographies.
3. Arbitration of commercial disputes between India and Pakistan.
4. Encyclopaedia of mathematics in French, German and Italian.
5. Standard editions of encyclopaedias in Zoology.
6. Cultural relations between France and USA.
7. Social conditions of primitive mountain dwellers in Kenya.
8. Hand book of Buddhist time reckoning.
9. Indias National Highway No. 19.
10. Annual report of Board of Control for Cricket in India (BCCI).
11. Organisation of steel industry in France in the 20th Century.
12. Wool for blankets making in Kashmir.
13. Working conditions female lawyers in U.K.
14. Translation of Russian novels in to Hindi.
15. Thermal effects of amplifiers.

Unit 6
Classification of Titles falling under the Main Classes 0/9

STRUCTURE

6.0. OBJECTIVES

In this unit an attempt has been made to classify simple, compound and complex titles with UDC-IME-93 falling under the main classes 0/9 and their principal divisions. After going through this unit you shall be able to :

* know the main classes and their principal divisions in UDC-IME-93.

* grasp and apply the directions and guidelines provided for at various places in the schedules and tables.
* classify simple, compound and complex titles falling under the main classes 0/9 and their divisions and subdivisions.
* analyse various facets of compound and complex subjects and build or synthesise the class number with the help of variety of common and special auxiliary tables and parallel divisions as well.

6.1. INTRODUCTION

In units 3 and 4 you have been introduced to the use and application of common and special auxiliary subdivisions for synthesising a class number. In unit 5 you have been introduced to the synthetic nature and number building process in UDC-IME-93. In this unit an attempt has been made to introduce you to the main classes and their principal divisions and select typical titles to cover some of these principal divisions. Each selected title has been analysed to show the appearance of facets and synthesising the facets with the respective notation taken from the schedules and/or tables and connecting the facets with respective connecting symbols so as to arrive at the coextensive class number.

The worked out examples under each of the main classes will provide you an idea as to the nature of the subject (titles) and the need to follow strictly the guidelines, directions and worked out examples found in the schedules and tables and the citation order to arrive at depth or minute class number.

6.2. GENERALITIES 0

The main divisions of this main class is as follows :

00 Prolegomena, Fundamentals of knowledge and culture.

01 Bibliography and bibliographies, catalogues.

02 Librarianship

030 Encyclopaedias, General reference works.

050 Serial publication, periodicals

06 Organisation, Associations, Congresses, Exhibitions, Museums.

07 News papers, Journalism, The press.

08 Polygraphies, collective works.

09 Manuscripts, Rare and remarkable works.

Worked out Examples

1. Standards in library and archive buildings.

Analysis

Standards in a special subject fields	006.44

Note : As per the worked out examples under 006.44 we have to add the number from architecture for library and archive buildings.

Library and Archive buildings	727.8	(to be added with :)

Synthesis

006.44 + : 727.8 = 006.44 : 727.8

2. Books in print

Analysis

Bibliographies	015
USA	(73)

Synthesis

015 + (73) = 015(73)

3. Decimal, Universal Decimal and Colon Classification, a study in Comparison.

Analysis

Decimal classification	025.4 DDC
Universal Decimal Classification	025.4 UDC
Colon Classification	025.47 CC

Synthesis

025.4 DDC + : 025.4 UDC + : 025.47 CC
= 025.4 DDC : 025.4 UDC : 025.47 CC

4. Ownership and control of periodicals in India.

Analysis

Periodicals	050	

Note : 050.1/.4 ≅ 070.1/.4

Ownership and control	070.2 i.e., 050.2	
India	(540)	from table Ie

Synthesis

050.2 + (540) = 050.2(540)

5. Indira Gandhi National Centre for Arts, New Delhi.

Analysis

Organisations for the advancement of culture	061.23	
Arts	7	(to be added with :)
Indira Gandhi National Centre for Arts	IGNCA	(alphabetical specification)
India	(540)	from table Ie

Synthesis

061.23 + : 7 + IGNCA + (540) = 061.23 : 7IGNCA (540)

6. Annual report of Salarjung Museum Hyderabad for the year 2005.

Analysis

Museums	069	
National	(1 - 4)	from table Ie
Annual report	(047)	from table Id
2005	"2005"	from table Ig

Synthesis

069 + (1 - 4) + (047) + "2005" = 069(1 - 4) (047) "2005"

7. Administrative report of Press Council of India.

Analysis

The press	070	
Commissions	061.24	(to be added with :)
Press council of India	PCI (alphabetical specification)	
India	(540)	from table Ie
Administrative report	(047.32)	from table Id

Synthesis

070 + : 061.24 + PCI + (540) + (047.32)
= 070 : 061.24 PCI (540) (047.32)

8. Catalogue of tamil palmleaf manuscripts.

Analysis

Manuscripts according to writing surface	091.2	
Writing surface	003.51	(to be added with :)
Note : Specify by	- 03	

Proceed to -03 at page 76.

Plant parts - 035.27 (page 77)

- 035.27 ≅ 631.57

Proceed to	631.57	at page 600
Leaves	631.57<u>4</u> i.e., -035.27<u>4</u>	
Tamil language	= 573.15	from table Ic
Catalogue	019.9	(to be added with :)

Synthesis

091.2 + - 035.274 + = 573.15 + : 019.9
= 091.2 - 035.274 = 573.15 : 019.9

9. The Best Books : A Readers Guide by W.S. Sonnenschein.

Analysis

Collective works	082	
Selected works	(081.2)	from table Id

Synthesis

082 + (081.2) = 082(081.2)

10. Guide to Reference Books by C.M. Winchell.

Analysis

Reference works	030	
Guide books	(036)	from table Id

Synthesis

030 + (036) = 030 (036)

Self Check Exercise - 1

Assign class numbers to the following titles.

1. Vikas catalogue, 2005.
2. AARC-II and CCC(5) : A comparative Study.
3. Australian National Bibliography.
4. Guide book on Brahmiscript Inscriptions.
5. Bibliography of Library Science Journals.
6. Union Catalogue of Social Science serials available in Academic Libraries in Andhra Pradesh.
7. Bibliography doctoral dissertation in sciences. 1950/2000.
8. Annual report of Indian Council for Cultural Relations.
9. Press in India : Annual Report of the Registrar of News Papers.
10. Bibliography of Paper Manuscripts.

Note :

(a) Write your answers in the space given below.

(b) Compare your answers with the model answers given at the end of this unit.

....

....

....

....

....

....

6.3. PHILOSOPHY. PSYCHOLOGY 1

The main divisions of this main class is as follows :

11 Metaphysics

13 Philosophy of mind and spirit. Metaphysics

14 Philosophical systems and points of view

159.9 Psychology

16 Logic, Epistemology, Theory of knowledge.

17 Moral philosophy, Ethics

Worked out Examples

1. Indian philosophy : An introductions to Hindu and Buddhist thought.

Analysis

Philosophy	1	
India	(540)	from table Ie
Hinduism	294.5	(to be added with :)
Buddhism	294.3	

Synthesis

1 + (540) + : 294.5 + + 294.3 = 1 (540) : 294.5 + 294.3

2. Philosophy of logic

Analysis

Logic	16	
Philosophy	1	(to be added with :)

Synthesis

16 + : 1 = 16 : 1

3. Introduction to physiological psychology.

Analysis

Psychology	159.9	
Physiology	612	(to be added with :)

Synthesis

159.9 + 612 = 159.9 : 612

4. Human personality in ancient Indian thought

Analysis

Personality (Human)	159.923	
Ancient India	934	(to be added with :)

Synthesis

159.923 + : 934 = 159.923 : 934

5. Encyclopaedia of ethics and logic

Analysis

Ethics	17	
Logic	16	
Encyclopaedia	(031)	from table Id

Synthesis

17 + + 16 + (031) = 17 + 16 (031)

6. Encyclopaedia of Indian Philosophers.

Analysis

Philosophy	1	
Biographies	929	(to be added with :)
Encyclopaedia	(031)	from table Id
India	(540)	from table Ie

Synthesis

1 + : 929 + (540) + (031) = 1 : 929(540)(031)

or

939 : 1(540) (031)

7. Industrial Psychology and organisational behaviour.

Analysis

Behaviour	159.9.019.4	
Industry	67	(to be added with :)

Synthesis

159.9.019.4 + : 67 = 159.9.019.4 : 67

8. Research on protection of animals of India.

Analysis

Protection of animals	179.3	
Research	.001.5	from table Ii
India	(540)	from table Ie

Synthesis

179.3 + .001.5 + (540) = 179.3.001.5 (540)

9. Illustrated guide book on astrology and palmistry.

Analysis

Astrology	133.52
Palmistry	133.6
Guide books	(036)
Illustrations	(0.025.2)

Synthesis

133.52 + + 133.6 + (036 + Ø.025.2)

= 133.52 + 133.6 (036.025.2)

10. Hand book of International psychology

Analysis

Psychology	159.9	
International	(100)	from table Ie
Hand book	(035)	from table Id

Synthesis

159.9 + (100) + (035) = 159.9 (100) (035)

Self Check Exercise - 2

Assign class number to the following titles.

1. An introduction to ethics for health professionals.
2. An introduction deductive logic.
3. Text book of abnormal psychology.
4. A dictionary of human behaviour.
5. Hand book of mental hygiene and the biological theories.

6. The quiet revolution in American Psychoanalysis.
7. Psychology of aggression, violence and crime.
8. A critical analysis of Kantian Philosophy.
9. The philosophy of Sri Bhagavad Gita.
10. Drug abuse and youth : A psychological study.

Note :

(a) Write your answers in the space given below.

(b) Compare your answers with the model answers given at the end of this unit.

....

....

....

....

....

....

....

....

....

6.4. RELIGION. THEOLOGY 2

The main divisions of this main class is as follows. The notation 22/28 is devoted to Christianity. Oriental religions is listed under 29.

21 Natural theology

22 The Bible, Holy scriptures

23/28 Christianity, The Christian religion

23 Dogmatic theology

24 Practical theology

25 Pastoral theology

26 Christian church in general

27 General history of the Christian church

28 Christian churches, sects, denominations

29 Non-Christian religions.

Worked out Examples

1. The Gospel of the Guru Granth Sahib.

Analysis

Sikhism	294.553
Sacred books	291.8

Synthesis

294.553 + 291.8 = 294.553.8

2. Hinduism, Buddhism and Jainism in ancient India.

Analysis

Hinduism	294.5	
Buddhism	294.3	
Jainism	294.35	
Ancient India	(34)	from table Ie

Synthesis

294.5 + + 294.3 + + 294.35 + (34)

= 294.5 + 294.3 + 294.35 (34)

3. Sathya Sai and his miraculous powers.

Analysis

Seets of Hinduism	294.55
Holy men	291.63

Synthesis

294.55 + 291.63 = 294.556.3

4. The cosmology of Rigveda

Analysis

Rigveda	294.118	
Cosmology	113/119	(to be added with :)

Synthesis

294.118 + : 113/119 = 294.118 : 113/119.

5. Religion and Society in the Himalayas.

Analysis

Religion	2	
Society	316.3	
Himalayas	(235.243)	from table Ie

Synthesis

2 + 316.3 + (235.243) = 2 + 316.3 (235.243)

6. The Arya Samaj : An account of its Origin, Doctrines and Activities.

Analysis

Sects of Hinduism	394.55	
Doctrines	291.2	
Arya Samaj	AS	(alphabetical specification)
Social reform organisations	061.235	
Activities	06.05	

Synthesis

294.55 + 291.2 + : 061.235 + AS + 06.05

= 294.55.2 : 061.235 AS .05

7. Medieval Muslim thinkers and scientists.

Analysis

Islam	297	
Thinkers	159.955 - 05	(to be added with :)
Scientists	5 - 05	(to be added with :)
Medieval period	"14"	from table Ig

Synthesis

297 + 159.955 - 05 + 5 - 05 + "14"

= 297 : 159.955 - 05 + 5 - 05 "14"

8. Jaina monuments of Orissa

Analysis

Jainism	294.35	
Monuments	725.94	(to be added with :)
Orissa	(541.5)	from table Ie

Synthesis

294.35 + : 725.94 + (541.5) = 294.35 : 725.94 (541.5)

9. Encyclopaedia of Saints of India.

Analysis

Holymen	291.6	
India	(540)	from table Ie
Encyclopaedia	(031)	from table Id

Synthesis

291.6 + (031) + (540) = 291.6(031) (540)

10. Socio-religious movements in British India.

Analysis

Religious organisation	291.6	
Sociology	316	(to be added with :)
British India	954.03	(to be added with :)

Synthesis

291.6 – : 316 + : 954.03 = 291.6 : 316 : 954.03

Self Check Exercise - 3

1. Religion, State and Politics in India.
2. The Rigvedic foundation of classical poetry.
3. Sikh shrines in Pakistan.
4. The language of Atharva Veda.
5. Ramayana theatre in India.
6. Religion, philosophy and literature of Bengal Vaishnavism.
7. The world of vedic life and culture.
8. Hindu manners, customs and Ceremonies.

9. The prophet : Life of Mohammad.
10. International Encyclopaedia of tribal re igion.

Note :

(a) Write your answers in the space given below.

(b) Compare your answers with the model answers given at the end of this unit.

....

....

....

....

....

....

....

....

....

....

....

....

....

6.5. SOCIAL SCIENCES 3

The main divisions of this main class is follows :

31 Demography, Sociology, Statistics.

32 Politics

33 Economics, Economic science

34 Law, Jurisprudence

35 Public administration, Military affairs.

36 Social work, Social aid, Housing, Insurance

37 Education, Teaching, Training, Leisure

389 Metrology, weights and measures

39 Ethnology, Customs, Folklore.

Worked out Examples

1. Research methodology in Social Sciences

Analysis

Methodology of Social Sciences	303.1
Feature of research	303.02

Synthesis

303.1 + 303.02 = 303.1.02

2. Family and Television : A sociological study

Analysis

Family	316.356.2
Television	621.397.122(to be added with :)

Synthesis

316.356.2 + : 621.397.122 = 316.356.2 : 621.397.122

3. Indo-Russian Relations : Prospects, Problems and Russia today.

Analysis

International relations	327	
India	(540)	from table Ie
Russia	(470)	from table Ie

Synthesis

327 + (540 : 470) = 327 (540 : 470)

4. Industrial growth and employment in India.

Analysis

Employment	331.5	
Industry	67	(to be added with :)
India	(540)	from table Ie

Synthesis

331.5 + : 67 + (540) = 331.5 : 67 (540)

5. Role of police in criminal justice system in India and Sri Lanka.

Analysis

Criminal justice (law)	343.1	
Police	351.74	(to be added with :)
India	(540)	from table Ie
Sri Lanka	(548.7)	from table Ie

Synthesis

343.1 + : 351.74 + (540 + 548.7)

= 343.1 : 351.74 (540 + 548.7)

6. Urban governance in North Eastern Region (India) : Legal issues and practices.

Analysis

Urban administration	353	
North Eastern Region (India)	(541)	from table Ie
Urban areas	(1 - 21)	from table Ie
Legal (issues)	34	(to be added with :)

Synthesis

353 + (543 - 1 - 21) + : 34 = 353(543 - 21) : 34

7. Directory of institutions involved in community work in India.

Analysis

Community work	364.46	
Institutions (Social work)	061.235	(to be added with :)
India	(540)	from table Ie
Directory	(058)	from table Id

Synthesis

364.46 + : 061.235 + (540) + (058)

= 364.46 : 061.235 (540) (058)

8. Finance and Management of Higher Education.

Analysis

Higher Education	378	
Finance	37.05	
Management	65	(to be added with :)

Synthesis

378 + 37.<u>05</u> + : 65 = 378.<u>05</u> : 65

9. A collection of wedding folksongs in Telugu.

Analysis

Folksongs	398.8	
Wedding (Customs)	392.5	(to be added with :)
Telugu	= 572.24	from table Ic
Collection	(08)	from table Id

Synthesis

398.8 + : 392.5 + = 572.24 + (08)

= 398.8 : 392.5 = 572.24 (08)

10. A dictionary of administrative and legislative terms

Analysis

Administration	35	
Legislature	328	(to be added with +)
Dictionary	(038)	

Synthesis

35 + + 328 + (038) = 35 + 328 (038)

Self Check Exercise - 4

Assign class numbers to the following titles.

1. Analytical methods for social research.
2. International Review of Sociography.
3. Women in Indian politics.
4. The economics of information technology.
5. Encyclopaedia of International terrorism.

6. District administration and training of officials in India.
7. Consumer advice centres and consumer protection in India.
8. Education, Nutrition and child development.
9. Folk festivals of Indians.
10. Dictionary of Kashmir proverbs and sayings.

Note :

(a) Write your answers in the space given below.

(b) Compare your answers with the model answers given at the end of this unit.

....

....

....

....

....

....

....

....

....

6.6. MATHEMATICS. NATURAL SCIENCES 5

The broad divisions of this main class is as follows :

51 Mathematics

52 Astronomy, Astrophysics, Space research

53 Physics

54 Chemistry, Crystallography

55 Earth sciences, Geology, Meteorology

56 Paleontology

57 Biological Sciences

58 Botany

59 Zoology

The schedules for the above subject fields have been

minutely enumerated and supported by variety of special auxiliary subdivisions. The following are worked out examples covering the above subject fields.

Worked out Examples

1. Number theory and its approach to cryptography

Analysis

Number theory	511.17	
Cryptography	003.26	(to be added with :)

Synthesis

511.7 + : 003.26 = 511.7 : 003.26

2. Statistical methods for Social science research workers.

Analysis

Statistical methods	519.22	
Research		
Scientific	001.891	(to be added with :)
Social Sciences	303	(to be added with :)
Workers	- 05	

Synthesis

519.22 + : 001.891 - 05 + 303 - 05
= 519.22 : 001.891 - 05 + 303 - 05

3. Annual report of Kodaikanal observatory.

Analysis

Observatories	520.1
Kodaikanal	(548.0 - 21 KODAI)
Annual report	(047.1)

Synthesis

520.1 + (548.1 - 21 KODAI) + (047.1)
= 520.1 (548.1 - 21 KODAI) (047.1)

4. Use of spacecraft for remote sensing.

Analysis

Remote sensing platform 528.837

Space craft 629.78 (to be added with :)

Synthesis

528.837 + : 629.78 = 528.837 : 629.78

5. Text book of Electricity and magnetism

Analysis

Electricity	537	
Magnetism	537.6	
Text book	(075)	

Synthesis

537 + 537.6 + (075) = 537 – 537.6 (075)

6. A text book of solid state physics and electronics.

Analysis

Solid state physics	538.9	
Electronics	537.5	
Text books	(075.9)	from table Id

Synthesis

538.9 + 537.5 + (075.8) = 538.9 + 537.5 (075.8)

7. Hand book of quantum chemistry including spectroscopy

Analysis

Quantum chemistry	544.18	
Spectroscopy	543.42	
Hand book	(035)	from table Id

Synthesis

544.18 + 543.42 + (035) = 544.18 + 543.42(035)

8. Proton impact of radiolysis

Analysis

Radiolysis	544.542.1	
Protons	539.125.4	(to be added with :)

Synthesis

544.542.1 + : 539.125.4 = 544.542.1 : 539.125.4

9. Research report on thermal energy from Bay of Bengal and Arabian Sea.

Analysis

Applied oceanography	551.46.09	
Hydrothermal energy	621.483	(to be added with :)
Bay of Bengal	(267.64)	from table Ie
Arabian Sea	(267.37)	from table Ie
Report	(047.31)	from table Id

Synthesis

551.46.09 + : 621.483 + (267.64 + 267.37) + (047.31)
= 551.46.09 : 621.483 (267.64 + 267.37) (047.31)

10. Footprints of crocodiles of Mesozoic period.

Analysis

Crocodiles	568.14	
Footprints	56.016.4	
Mesozoic period	"615"	from table Ig

Synthesis

568.14 + 56.016.4 + "615" = 568.14.016.4 "615"

11. Theoretical aspects of chemical and biological factors of cytoplasm.

Analysis

Cytoplasm	576.311	
Chemical factors	57.044	
Biological factors	57.047	
Theoretical aspects (Point of view)	.001	from table Ii

Synthesis

576.31 + 57.044 + 57.047 + .001 = 576.31.044.047.001

12. Variations in Pigmentation in rosales due to weather

Analysis

Rosales	582.71	
External characteristics and traits	58.018	
Variations in pigmentation	57.0186.6	

Note : 58.018 ≅ 57.018

Weather	551.515	(to be added with :)

Synthesis

582.71 + 58.018 + ~~57.01~~8.6 + : 551.515
= 582.71.018.6: 551.515

13. Annual report of Botanical Survey of India.

Analysis

Botany	58	
Organisations for the advancement of Science	061.23	(to be added with :)
Botanical Survey of India	BSI (alphabetical specification)	
Annual report	(047.3)	from table Id

Synthesis

58 + : 061.23 + BSI + (047.3) = 58 : 061.23 BSI (047.3)

14. Illustrated hand book of Tiger sanctuaries in North East India.

Analysis

Tigers	599.742.71	
Sanctuaries	502.742	(to be added with :)
India	(540)	from table Ie
North-East	(1 - 18)	from table Ie

Synthesis

599.742.71 + :502.742 + (540 + *1* - 18) + (035 + 0.025.2)
= 599.742.71:502.742(540 - 18) (035.025.2)

15. Protection of black vultures in South Asia

Analysis

Black vultures	598.912	
Protection of animals	502.743	(to be added with :)
Asia	(5)	from table Ie
South	(1 - 13)	from table Ie

Synthesis

598.912 + : 502.743 + (5 + *1* - 13)

= 598.912 : 502.743(5 - 13)

Self Check Exercise - 5

Assign class number to the following titles :

1. Annual report of National Chemical laboratory, Pune.
2. Depletion of Ironore deposits in Australia.
3. Measures in conservation by draining waste in engineering.
4. Encyclopaedia of polymer science engineering.
5. Imprints of palms of fossils of palaezoic period.
6. Saturn satellite IV.
7. Theory of surfaces of differential geometry in symplectic spaces.
8. Raman effect and light scattering.
9. Field experiments on Himalayan glaciers.
10. Pathological biochemistry of microorganism.
11. Climatic effects on flowers, fruits and seeds.
12. Survey of high mountain hawks in India.
13. Indian law against hunting and capturing animals.
14. Biochemistry of plants.
15. Electrosynthesis of potassium chloride.

Note :

(a) Write your answers in the space given below.

(b) Compare your answers with the model answers given at the end of this unit.

....

....

....

....

....

....

....

....

6.7. APPLIED SCIENCES. MEDICINE. TECHNOLOGY 6

The schedules for Applied sciences, Medicine and Technology have been very minutely drawn to meet the everchanging needs of user libraries. More than 450 pages of schedules have been devoted to various branches Applied sciences, Medicine and Technology. The broad divisions of the above main classes is as follows :

61 Medical Sciences

62 Engineering, Technology in general

63 Agriculture, Forestry, Farming

64 Home economics, Domestic science, House keeping

65 Management, Trade, Communication

66 Chemical technology, Chemical and Related industries

67 Various industries, trades and crafts

68 Industries, crafts and trades for finished or assembled articles

69 Building (Construction) trade.

All the three types of special auxiliaries tables viz. 1. hyphen series, point nought series and apostrophe series have been provided at various places in the schedules which have greatly enhanced the synthetic quality of notation in UDC. The following worked out examples shall amply demonstrate this quality.

Worked out Examples

1. X-ray diagnosis and surgical treatment of lung cancer.

Analysis

Lungs	616.24
Cancer	616 - 006
X-ray diagnosis	616 - 073.7
Surgical treatment	616 - 089

Synthesis

616.24 + ***616*** - 006 + ***616*** - 073.7 + ***616*** - 089
= 616.24 - 006 - 073.7 - 089

2. History of Indian Council for Medical Research (ICMR), New Delhi.

Analysis

Medicine	61	
Organisation for the advancement of knowledge/Science	061.22	(to be added with :)
Indian council for Medical Research	ICMR	(alphabetical specification)
India	(540)	from table le
History	(09)	from table Id

Synthesis

61 + : 061.22 + ICMR + (540) + (09)
= 61 : 061.22 ICMR (540) (09)

3. Student's Manual of Direct current machines with regulation by means of transformers

Analysis

Direct current machines	621.313.2
Regulation by transformers	621.3.077.4
Manual	(035)

Synthesis

621.313.2 + 621.3.077.4 + (035) = 621.313.2.077.4(035)

4. Working chambers for X-ray apparatus in Hospitals

Analysis

X-ray apparatus	621.386.8	
Working chambers	62-784.5	
Hospitals	61 : 061	(to be added with :)

Synthesis

621.386.8 + 62 - 784.5 + : 61 : 061

= 621.386.8 - 784.5 : 61 : 061

or

621.386.8 - 784.5 : 725.51

5. Honey bee diseases and their management

Analysis

Honey bee diseases 638.15

Note : 638.15 - 02/-099 General pathology of bees 638.15 - 02/-099 ≅ 616 - 02/-099.

Administration of treatment 616 - 082

Synthesis

638.15 + 616 - 082 = 638.15 - 082

6. Malnutrition and treatment of Vegetable crops in India.

Analysis

Vegetable crops 635.1/.8

Note : 635 - 1 - 2 Plant damage and disease

635 - 1 / -2 ≅ 631/632

Control of plant diseases 632.93 i.e., 635 - 93

Synthesis

635.1/.8 + 635 - 93 = 635.1/.8 - 93

7. Text book of Food Nutrition, Child care and Psychology.

Analysis

Food nutrition	613.2	
Child care	649.1	
Psychology	159.9	(to be added with :)
Text book	(075)	from table Id

Synthesis

613.2 + 649.1 + : 159.9 + (075)

= 613.2 + 649.1 : 159.9 (075)

8. Dictionary of Food technology and human nutrition

Analysis

Food technology	641	
Human nutrition	613.2	(to be added with :)
Dictionary	(038)	from table Id

Synthesis

641 + : 613.2 + (038) = 641 : 613.2 (038)

9. Administration and Management of Electricity in India.

Analysis

Management	65	
Administration	35	
Electricity	621.31	(to be added with :)
India	(540)	from table Ie

Synthesis

65 + 35 + : 621.31 + (540) = 65 + 35 : 621.31 (540)

10. Management of small scale industries in India.

Analysis

Management	65	
Small scale industries	334.713	(to be added with :)
India	(540)	from table Ie

Synthesis

65 + : 334.713 + (540) = 65 : 334.713 (540)

11. Marketing of Surf soap powder in India.

Analysis

Soap powder	661.187 - 492	
Surf	SURF	(alphabetical specification)
Marketing	658.8	(to be added with :)
India	(540)	from table Ie

Synthesis

661.187 - 492 + SURF + : 658.8 + (540)
= 661.187 - 492SURF : 658.8(540)

12. Illustrated hand book of Preservation of mangoes by gases.

Analysis

Fruits preserved by particular method 664.853

Note : Denote the kind of fruit by : 634...

664.853 ≅ 664.8.03

Food preserved by gases	664.8.035 1	
Hand book	(035)	
Illustrations	(0.025.2)	
mangoes	634.441	(to be added with :)

Synthesis

664.853 + 664.8.035.1 − : 634.441 + (035 + 0.025.2)
= 664.853.51 : 634.441 (035.025.2)

13. A brochure on exhibition of Nizam's Jewelry by Salarjung Museum of Hyderabad.

Analysis

Specialised exhibitions	061.43	(to be added with :)
Jewelry	671.12	
Royalty	923.731	(to be added with :)

Nizams	NIZAM (alphabetical specification)	
Hyderabad	(548.4 - 25 HYD)	
Brochure	(041)	from table Id

Synthesis

671.12+:923.71+NIZAM+(548.4-25HYD)+(041)+:061.4
= 671.12 : 923.71 NIZAM (548.4 - 25 HYD) (041) : 061.4

or

061.4 : 671.12 : 923.71 NIZAM (548.4 - 25 HYD) (041)

14. Introduction to Electrophotography printers.

Analysis

Non-impact printers 681.625.92

Note : Denote particulars of processes not listed here by :
77 ... (P. 809)

Electrophotography 777.932

Synthesis

681.625.92 + : 777.932 = 681.625.92 : 777.932

15. Light metal-framed partitions for hospital buildings.

Analysis

Framed partitions 692.253

Note : Denote framing materials by :
639 ... : 694 ... (P. 839)

Light metal	693.977	(to be added with :)
Hospital buildings	725.511	(to be added with :)

Synthesis

692.253 + : 693.977 + : 725.511
= 692.253 : 693.977 : 725.511

Self Check Exercise - 6

Assign class numbers to the following titles.

1. Herbal medicine for human diseases.
2. Every one's guide to cancer therapy.

3. A manual of practical Engineering Chemistry.
4. Surface engineering and heat treatment past, present and future.
5. Mechanical and electrical systems in construction and architecture
6. Traditional agriculture and water technology in Eastern Uttar Pradesh.
7. Agricultural dictionary of Scientific and Technical abbreviations.
8. Practical manual for agricultural chemistry.
9. Text book of home management, Hygiene and Physiology.
10. Hotel management and Hospitality enterprises.
11. Electric power supply in Mumbai city.
12. Twisted cotton yarn threads.
13. Sales promotion policy for precision watches and clocks.
14. Costing of optical flint glass fibres.

Note :

(a) Write your answers in the space given below.

(b) Compare your answers with the model answers given at the end of this unit.

....

....

....

....

....

....

....

....

....

....

....

....

6.8. THE ARTS. RECREATION. ENTERTAINMENT. SPORT 7

The main class includes various fine arts, sports, recreation and entertainment and also architecture. The main divisions of this main class is as follows :

71 Physical planning, Regional, Town and Country planning

72 Architecture

73 Plastic arts

74 Drawing, Design, Applied arts and crafts

75 Painting

76 Graphic arts, Graphics

77 Photography

78 Music

79 Recreation, Entertainment, Games, Sport

All the above divisions and their subdivisions are well supported by special auxiliary subdivisions especially point nought series. The following worked out example will demonstrate the synthetic nature of UDC notation.

Worked out Examples

1. Art and architecture of Uttar Pradesh.

Analysis

Art	7	
Architecture	72	
Uttar Pradesh	(545.8)	from table Ie

Synthesis

7 ÷ 72 + (545.8) = 7 + 72(545.8)

2. Art and antiquities of India, an illustrated selection.

Analysis

Art	7	
Antiquities	904	
Illustrations	(0.025.4)	from table Id

India	(540)	from table Ie

Synthesis

7 + 904 + (540) + (0.025.4) = 7 + 904 (540) (0.025.4)

3. Hand book of gold coins of Mogal period in India.

Analysis

Coins	737.1	
Gold	73.023.3	
India	(540)	from table Ie
Mogal period	"14/16"	from table Ig
Hand book	(035)	from table Id

Synthesis

737.1 + 73.<u>023.3</u> + (540) + (035) + "14/16"
= 737.<u>023.3</u> (540) (035) "14/16"

4. Manual of decoration of bed rooms.

Analysis

Interior decoration	747	
Bed rooms	643.515	(to be added with :)
Manual	(035)	from table Id

Synthesis

474 + : 643.515 + (035) = 747 : 643.515 (035)

5. Water colour paintings of Pablo Piccasso

Analysis

Painting	75	
Water color	75.021.322	
Pablo piccasso	Piccasso	(alphabetical specification)

Synthesis

75 + 75.<u>021.322</u> + Piccasso = 75.021.322 Piccasso

6. Religions subjects in Indian Painting

Analysis

Subjects for Painting	75.04

Note : For subdivisions see 7.04 ... Religions subjects 7.046.3 (P. 853)

India	(540)

Synthesis

75.04 + 7.046.3 + (540) = 75.046.3(540)

7. Advertising on match boxes as commercial graphics.

Analysis

Commercial graphics	766
Advertising on particular objects	659.136.1
Match boxes	662.536.2

Synthesis

766 + : 659.136.1 + : 662.536.2
= 766 : 659.136.1 : 662.536.2

8. Developing equipment for photographs for rail traffic accidents.

Analysis

Developing equipment	771.43	
News photography	77.044	
Rail traffic accidents	656.2.08	(to be added with :)

Synthesis

771.43 + : 77.044 + : 656.2.08 = 771.43 : 77.044 : 656.2.08

9. Sounds of the sacred hindu religions music in India.

Analysis

Religions music	783 ·	
Hinduism	294.5	(to be added with :)
India	(540)	from table Ie

Synthesis

783 + : 294.5 + (540) = 783:294.5(540)

10. Music of U. Srinivas, famous mandolin player.

Analysis

Mandolin	787.65	
U. Srinivas	'Srinivas'	(alphabetical specification)

Synthesis

787.65 + Srinivas = 787.6Srinivas

11. Stage design for telugu shadow plays.

Analysis

Shadow plays	792.96	
Stage design	792.021	
Telugu	= 572.24	from table Ic

Synthesis

792.96 + 792.021 + =572.24 = 792.96.021 = 572.24

12. Encyclopaedia of sports and games.

Analysis

Sports	796
Games	794
Encyclopaedia	(031)

Synthesis

796 + + 794 + (031) = 796 + 794(031)

13. Guide book of roller skating manoeuvers.

Analysis

Roller skating	796.691	
Manoeuvers	796.054.4	
Guide books	(036)	from table Id

Synthesis

796.691 + 796.054.4 + (036) = 796.691.054.4 (036)

14. Hawk racing in Saudi Arabia.

Analysis

Animal contest	798.9

Hawk	598.915	(to be added with :)
Saudi Arabia	(532)	from table Ie

Synthesis

798.9 + : 598.915 + (532) = 798.9 : 598.915(532)

15. Rules and regulations of Bangalore race club.

Analysis

Horse racing	798.4	
Sports club	061.237	(to be added with :)
Rules and regulation	796.063	
Bangalore	(548.2 - 25 BAN)	

Synthesis

798.4 + 796.063 : 061.237 + (548.2 - 25 BAN)
= 798.4.063 : 061.237(548.2 - 25 BAN)

Self Check Exercise - 7

Assign class numbers to the following titles.

1. Hand book of Indian Architecture.
2. Summer resorts of South India.
3. The maritime and Coastal forts of India.
4. Buddhist sculpture and Iconography.
5. Collection of political cartoons from Hindu News Paper.
6. Economic and Social aspects of performing Arts in China.
7. Human anatomy for artists.
8. Dictionary of Western Church music.
9. Tribal paintings and sculptures.
10. History of post renaissance painting in France.
11. Tribal melodies of Himachal Pradesh.
12. Classification of photographic systems.
13. Production of artistic films in India.
14. Script writers for Marathi spiritual plays.
15. Long distance under water swimming.
16. Satish Gujral : An artography.

Note :

(a) Write your answers in the space given below.

(b) Compare your answers with the model answers given at the end of this unit.

....

....

....

....

....

....

....

....

....

....

....

....

....

6.9. LANGUAGE. LINGUISTICS. LITERATURE 8

As stated already Language and Linguistics earlier provided for at 4 has been transformed to 8. The digit 4 has been frozen for the time being. The main divisions and subdivisions of language, linguistics and literature has been enumerated under 80/821. The main divisions are as follows :

80 General questions

81 Linguistics and languages

82 Literature.

In the schedules we find the provision of hyphen and apostrophe series of special auxiliary subdivisions. The following worked out examples demonstrate the use of these two types of special auxiliary subdivisions.

Worked out Examples

1. A grammar of classical Arabic Language.

Analysis

Arabic language	811.411.21
Classical period	81'02
Grammar	81'36

Synthesis

811.411.21 + 81'02 + 81'36 = 811.411.21'02 '36

2. Historical survey of Ancient Indian Grammars : Sanskrit, Pali & Prakrit.

Analysis

Sanskrit	811.211	
Prakrit	811.213	
Pali	811.212	
Grammar	81'36	
History	(09)	from table Id
Ancient India	(34)	from table Ie

Synthesis

811.211/.213 + 81'36 + (34) + (09)

= 811.211/.213'36 (34) (09)

or

811.211'36 + 811.213'36 + 811.212'36(34) (09)

3. An outline of English phonetics.

Analysis

English language	811.111	
Phonetics	81'342	
Outlines	.001.13	from table Ii

Synthesis

811.111 + 81'342 + .001.13 = 811.111 '342 .001.13

4. A Historical Grammar of Inscriptional Telugu

Analysis

Telugu language	811.572.25	
Grammar	81'36	
Inscriptions	930.27	(To be added with :)
History	(09)	from table Id

Synthesis

811.572.25 + 81'36 + : 930.27 + (09)

= 811.572.25'36 : 930.27 (09)

5. The year book of South Asian Languages and Linguistics, 1999.

Analysis

Language and Linguistics	81	
South Asia	(540 - 13)	
Year book	(058)	from table Id
1999	"1999"	from table Ig

Synthesis

81 + (540 - 13) + (058) + "1999"

= 81 (540 - 13) (058) "1999"

6. Language, Education and Society.

Analysis

Language	81	
Education	37	(to be added with :)
Society	316.3	

Synthesis

81 + : 37 + 316.3 = 81 : 37 + 316.3

7. An International Bibliography of Dravidian Languages and Linguistics.

Analysis

Dravidian languages	811.57

Bibliography	016	(to be added with :)
International	(100)	from table Ie

Synthesis

811.57 + : 016 + (100) = 811.57 : 016(100)

8. Bharati's Longer Poems, a selection

Analysis

Tamil Literature	821.573.15	
Poetry	82 - 1	
Selection	(081.2)	

Synthesis

821.573.15 + 82 - 1 + (081.2) = 821.573.15 - 1 (081.2)

9. Studies in contemporary Indian English Drama.

Analysis

English literature	821.111	
Indian	(540)	from table Ie
Drama	82 - 2	
Contemporary	"654"	from table Ig

Synthesis

821.111 + (540) + 82 - 2 + "654" = 821.111(540) - 2 "654"

10. Hinduism in T.S. Elliots writings.

Analysis

English literature	821.111	
T.S. Elliot	Elliot	(alphabetical specification)
Hinduism	294.5	(to be added with :)

Synthesis

821.111 Elliot + : 294.5 = 821.111 Elliot : 294.5

11. A collection of poems of Kabir translated in to English.

Analysis

Hindi literature	821.214.21	

Poetry	82 - 1	
Kabir	Kabir (alphabetical specification)	
Collection	(081.1)	from table Id
Translations	= 03	from table Ic
English language	= 111	from table Ic

Synthesis

821.214.21 + 82 - 1 + KABIR + (081.1) + = 03 + = 111

= 821.214.21 - 1 Kabir (081.1) = 03 = 111

12. Gurazada Appa Rao : Kanya Sulkam, Telugu drama.

Analysis

Telugu literature	821.572.24
Drama	82 - 2
Gurazada Appa Rao	Appa Rao (alphabetical specification)
Kanya Sulkam (Individual works)	7 KAN (alphabetical specification)

Synthesis

821.572.24 + 82 - 2 + Appa Rao + KAN

= 821.572.24 - 2 + Appa Rao 7KAN

Self Check Exercise - 8

Assign class number to the following titles.

1. Rogets thesaurus of English words and phrases.
2. Teaching spoken English and communication skills.
3. Tribal linguistics in India : A bibliographical survey.
4. General and comparative Dravidian languages and linguistics.
5. Modern English Grammar with practical Exercises.
6. Indian English Fiction : an assessment.
7. Kamala Markandaya : A critical study of her Novels, 1954/1982.
8. C. Nayana Reddy : Vishwambhara, a Poetical work.

9. The Davinci Code by Dan Brown.
10. The Literary Semantics of Kalidasa.
11. Mundari Grammar and Exercises.
12. Ancient Sanskrit Literature and Human Resource Development.

Note :

(a) Write your answers in the space given below.

(b) Compare your answers with the model answers given at the end of this unit.

....

....

....

....

....

....

....

6.10. GEOGRAPHY. BIOGRAPHY. HISTORY 9

The broad division of this main class is as follows :

902/904	Archaeology, Prehistory.
908	Area studies, Study of locality
91	Geography, Exploration, Travel, Regional Geography
929	Biographical and related studies
93/99	History
930	Science of history in general
931	Ancient history in general
94	Medieval and modern history.

In the schedules for the above divisions and subdivisions we find the provision point nought and apostrophe series of special auxiliary subdivisions. The following worked out examples will demonstrate the use of these special auxiliary subdivisions in the synthesis or number building process in UDC.

Worked out Examples

1. Annual Report of Archaeological Survey of India for the year 2005.

Analysis

Archaeology	902	
Archaeological Survey of India	ASI (alphabetical specification)	
Learned organisations	061.22	(to be added with :)
Annual Report	(047.1)	from table Id
India	(540)	from table Id
2005	"2005"	from table Ig

Synthesis

902 + : 061.22 + ASI + (540) + (047.1) + "2005"
= 902 : 061.22 ASI (540) (047.1) "2005"

2. Burial remains of pre-historic cultures found in Gangetic valley

Analysis

Burial remains	903.5	
Pre-historic cultures	903'1	
Ganges	(282.253.21)	from table Ie
Valley	(23.04)	

Synthesis

903.5 + ~~903~~'1 + (282.253.21 + 23.04)
= 903.5'1 (282.253.21.04)

3. Regional Geography of the world

Analysis

Regional Geography	913	
World	(100)	from table Ie

Synthesis

913 + (100) = 913(100)

4. India : An Economic and Commercial Geography

Analysis

Human Geography	911.3	
Economics	33	(to be added with :)
Commerce	339	
India	(540)	

Synthesis

911.3 + : 33 + 339 + (540) = 911.3 : 33 + 339 (540)

5. Travel Industry and Tourism in India.

Analysis

Travels	910.4	
Industry	67	(to be added with :)
Tourism	379.85	
India	(540)	from table Ie

Synthesis

910.4 + :67 + : 379.85 + (540) = 910.4:67 : 379.85 (540)

6. An account of travels between ancient China and India.

Analysis

Travels	910.4	
Ancient India	(34)	from table Ie
Ancient China	(31)	from table Ie

Synthesis

910.4 + (34 : 31) = 910.4 (34 : 31)

7. Encyclopaedia of Indian biography

Analysis

Biography	929	
India	(540)	from table Ie
Encyclopaedia	(031)	from table Ie

Synthesis

929 + (540) + (031) = 929 (540) (031)

8. Scientist to President Dr. A.P.J. Abdul Kalam.

Analysis

Biography	929	
A.P.J. Abdul Kalam	Kalam	(alphabetical specification)

Synthesis

929 + Kalam = 929 Kalam

9. The History and culture of Indian People

Analysis

Indian History	954
Culture	008

Synthesis

954 + 008 = 954 + 008

10. Fashion Styles of ancient India.

Analysis

Ancient India	934	
Fashion	391	(to be added with :)

Synthesis

934 + : 391 = 934 : 391

11. Archival material on British India's relations with Great Britain

Analysis

British India	954.03	
Gt. Britain	941	(to be added with :)
Archives	930.25	(to be added with :)

Synthesis

954.03 + : 941 + : 930.25 + : 930.25

= 954.03 : 941 : 930.25

12. Research reports of Indian Council for Historical Research.

Analysis

History	9

Learned Society	061.22	(to be added with :)
Indian Council for Historical Research	ICHR (alphabetical specification)	
India	(540)	from table Ie
Research reports	(047.31)	from table Id

Synthesis

9 + : 061.22 + ICHR + (540) + (047.31)
= 9 : 061.22 ICHR (540) (047.31)

Self Check Exercise - 9

Assign class numbers to the following titles.

1. Exploration of Himalayan glaciers.
2. Biography eminent Indian Nuclear Scientists.
3. Fundamentals of Animal geography.
4. Computing Mathematical techniques in Geography.
5. Application of Geography to wide life conservation.
6. Archaeology in Orissa : Sites and monuments.
7. India and the common wealth : a bibliography.
8. Aspects of Ancient Indian polity.
9. The agrarian system of Mogal India.
10. Coats of arms of British India.
11. Archeometallurgy in ancient India.
12. Battles of Medieval India (A.D. 1296 - 1850)

Note :

(a) Write your answers in the space given below.

(b) Compare your answers with the model answers given at the end of this unit.

....

....

....

....

....

6.11. SUMMARY

In the proceedings sections of this unit an attempt has been made to classify macro documents falling under the main classes 0/9 with UDC. These worked out examples amply demonstrate the need for using various common and special auxiliary tables and parallel divisions for synthesising a class number. The worked out examples will also provide you an idea as to the synthetic nature of notation in UDC to arrive at coextensive class number. The self check exercises provided at the end of worked out examples for each main class will provide you more practice for classifying various types of documents with the help of UDC-IME-1993.

6.12. ANSWERS TO SELF CHECK EXERCISES

Exercise - 1

1. 018.4 Vikas "2005"
2. 025.31AACR : 025.31 CCC
3. 015(94)
4. 003.336.3 : 930.271(036)
5. 016 : 02(05)
6. 017.11 : 3(05) : 027.7 (548.23)
7. 016 : 5 (043.3) "1950/2000"
8. 061.22 : 008ICCR (540) (047)
9. 070 : 351(540)(058) (047)
10. 091.2 : 003.51

Exercise - 2

1. 17 : 614-05
2. 162.2
3. 159.97(0.06)
4. 159.929(038)
5. 159.913.015.7(035)
6. 159.964.2.001.55(73)

7. 159.9 : 316.485.26 : 316.625
8. 1KANT(049.32)
9. 1 : 294.118
10. 159.9 : 343.575 + 316.346.32 - 316

Exercise - 3

1. 2 : 341.211 : 32(540)
2. 294.118 : 82 - 1'02
3. 294.553.35 (549.1)
4. 294.118 : 81
5. 294.518 : 792(540)
6. 2 : 1 : 8 : 294.5(541.2)
7. 294.114 : 008
8. 294.513.7
9. 297.163 : 929 or 929 Muhammad
10. 2 : 57.063.6(031)

Exercise - 4

1. 303.833.5
2. 308(051)
3. 32 : 396(540)
4. 33 : 681.518
5. 323.28 (100) (031)
6. 353.5.088.6 (540)
7. 366.61.07 : 366.5(540)
8. 37 : 613.22 + 649.1
9. 394.2 (= 1.540)
10. 398.91 = 214.2(038)

Exercise - 5

1. 54 : 061.22 NCL(540) (047.1)
2. 504.55.052 : 553.31(94)

3. 504.064 : 658.567.5
4. 541.+ 62(031)
5. 561.545.012.3"613"
6. 523.46 - 87 * 4
7. 514.756.44
8. 535.375.5 : 535.36
9. 551.324.005 (235.243)
10. 579.61 : 616 - 008.9 - 092.8
11. 581.46/.48.056
12. 598.915 (540 + 23.03)
13. 591.611 : 34 (540)
14. 579.22 : 58
15. 554.653.1 : 546.32'131

Exercise - 6

1. 616 : 613.291 or 613.291 : 616
2. 616 - 006.6 - 08(036)
3. 62 : 54.002 (035)
4. 62 - 408 : 621.78 "311/313"
5. 621 + 621.3 : 69 + 72
6. 631 + 628.14 (545.8 - 11)
7. 63(038) : 5 + 6 : 003.083
8. 63 : 54 (035)
9. 64 : 613 + 612
10. 65 : 640.41 + 649.9
11. 66.013.6 : 621.311 (547.1 MAH - 25 MUMBAI)
12. 677.21.072.022.6
13. 681.11 - 187.4 : 658.82.011.1
14. 692.44 : 726.1
15. 666.189.21 : 666.221.4.034

Exercise - 7

1. 72(540)(035)
2. 711.455(540 - 13) "322"
3. 725.182 (540 + 210.5)
4. 730 : 294.3 : 73.04
5. 741.5 : 32 (054 Hindu) (08)
6. 79 : 33 + 301(51)
7. 743 : 61 : 7 - 051
8. 783(1 - 15) (038)
9. 75 + 730 : 572.9 or 572.9 : 75 + 730
10. 75.035(44)
11. 78 : 57.063.6(545.4)
12. 773.026.63 : 025.4
13. 791.43.05 : 7(540)
14. 799.225.071.1 = 214.315
15. 797.215.093.38
16. 929 : 75 or 929 Gujral (540)

Exercise - 8

1. 811.11'373.4'373.7 (038)
2. 811.111'271.16 + 316.28:37

   or

   37 : 811.111'271.16 + 316.28
3. 81 (= 081) (540) : 016
4. 811.57 - 115
5. 811.111'06'36.004.14
6. 821.111(540) - 3(09)
7. 821.111 KAMAL - 3(09) "1954/1982"
8. 821.572.24 - 1NAR 7 VIS
9. 821.111 - 3BRO 7 Davinci

10. 811.221 - 3 ‘37
11. 811.613.6‘36.004.14
12. 811.221‘01 : 331.101.262

Exercise - 9

1. 910.3 : 551.324 (235.243)
2. 929 : 539.1 (540)
3. 911.2 : 591.9
4. 91 : 51.3
5. 911.9 : 502.7
6. 902.2 + 903.6 (541.5)
7. 954(1 - 41) : 016
8. 934 : 32
9. 954.02 : 338.431“1526/1717”
10. 954.03 : 929.6
11. 902 : 669(934)
12. 954 “1295/1850” : 355.48

6.13. ASSIGNMENT

Classify the following titles using UDC(IME-93)

1. Indian Library Refresher; a quarterly journal on Indian Publications Published by Ess Ess Publications, 2005.
2. Oriental manuscripts world wide.
3. Documentary heritage of Indian Libraries.
4. Objective Question Banks for Library and Information Science Ability Text.
5. Jute cultivation of India.
6. Fundamentals of Environmental Biology.
7. Systematic Botany : Taxonomy of Angiosperm.
8. The saga of Sri Satya Sai Baba.
9. Elements of Industrial Chemistry.
10. Labour problems and Labour welfare.

11. Industrial Management & Production Management and Operation Research.
12. Fundamentals of programming and information technology.
13. Indian Industrial Development.
14. A text book of Health & Physical Education.
15. Art and Science of Metal Casting.
16. Yoga for Better Living and Self-Realization
17. Races and culture of India.
18. A Text book of stratigraphy, Micropaleontology and Paleobotany.
19. Text books on Food storage and preservation.
20. Heritage of Indian Art and Architecture.
21. On ten plays of Shakespeare.
22. A. Bapi Raju : Narayana Rao (Telugu Novel)
23. Better Thesis Writing
24. Better Pediatric Prescribing
25. Solution of Business Mathematics and Statistics.
26. Fundamentals of Physical Education.
27. Essentials of mathematical physics
28. Indian Government and Policies.
29. Experiments and Tests in Psychology.
30. Activities of International whaling commission.
31. Annual Report of Dept. of Atomic Energy, Govt. of India.
32. Asbestos : Home construction.
33. Cryptography in E-voting.
34. Water haycinth : Vermi Compost.
35. Managing Honey bee colonies.
36. National centre for Antarctica and Ocean Research.
37. Rules and Regulations of International Cricket Council.

38. The sounds of world's languages.
39. Persecuting Jews during Nazi Germany.
40. A text book on Pharmaceutical analysis.
41. Text book of Veterinary Gynaecology, Artificial insemination and Assisted Reproduction.
42. Charles Dickens : A tale of two cities.
43. The empowerment of women of India.
44. Children, Law and Justice.
45. Encyclopaedia of Petroleum sciences and Engineering.
46. The Encyclopaedia of District Gazetteers of India.
47. Glossary of Drama Theatre and Electronic Media : English - Hindi.
48. Illustrated Encyclopaedia of Reptiles of India.
49. Index of Songs in South Indian Music.
50. Ranganathan Dictionary : Indian Terminology on Library and Information Science.

6.14. SELECTED READINGS

The following sources will help you to know more about theory and practice of UDC.

1. Guide to Universal Decimal Classification (UDC) B.S. 1000 C. 1963. London, BSI, 1963.
2. Mills, J. The Universal Decimal Classification. V.I. Rutgers Graduate School of Library Services. New Brunswick, New Jersey, 1964.
3. McIlwaine, I.C. Guide to the use of the Universal Decimal Classification, London, BSI, 1993.
4. Raju, A.A.N. Universal Decimal Classification (IME, 1985) : A practical and Self Instructional Manual. Madras, T.R. Publications, 1991.
5. Universal Decimal Classification, International Medium Edition. English Text Part-1. Systematic Tables, 1985.